What people are saying

"Here at Citibank we use the Quick Course® computer training book series for 'just-in-time' job aids—the books are great for users who are too busy for tutorials and training. Quick Course® books provide very clear instruction and easy reference."

Bill Moreno, Development Manager
Citibank
San Francisco, CA

"At Geometric Results, much of our work is PC related and we need training tools that can quickly and effectively improve the PC skills of our people. Early this year we began using your materials in our internal PC training curriculum and the results have been outstanding. Both participants and instructors like the books and the measured learning outcomes have been very favorable."

Roger Hill, Instructional Systems Designer
Geometric Results Incorporated
Southfield, MI

"The concise and well organized text features numbered instructions, screen shots, and useful quick reference pointers, and tips…[This] affordable text is very helpful for educators who wish to build proficiency."

Computer Literacy column
Curriculum Administrator Magazine
Stamford, CT

"I have purchased five other books on this subject that I've probably paid more than $60 for, and your [Quick Course®] book taught me more than those five books combined!"

Emory Majors
Searcy, AR

"I would like you to know how much I enjoy the Quick Course® books I have received from you. The directions are clear and easy to follow with attention paid to every detail of the particular lesson."

Betty Weinkauf, Retired Senior
Mission, TX

QUICK COURSE®

in

MICROSOFT®

PUBLISHER 2000

ONLINE PRESS INC.

Microsoft®*Press*

PUBLISHED BY
Microsoft Press
A Division of Microsoft Corporation
One Microsoft Way
Redmond, WA 98052-6399

Library of Congress Cataloging-in-Publication Data

Quick Course in Microsoft Publisher 2000 / Online Press Inc.
     p.   cm.
  Includes index.
  ISBN 1-57231-990-9
  1. Microsoft Publisher.   2. Desktop publishing.   I. Online Press
Inc.
  Z253.532.M53Q53   1999
  686.2'25445369 - - dc21   98-55329
                                                  CIP

Printed and bound in the United States of America.

2 3 4 5 6 7 8 9   WCWC   4 3 2 1 0 9

Distributed in Canada by Penguin Books Canada Limited.

A CIP catalogue record for this book is available from the British Library.

Microsoft Press books are available through booksellers and distributors worldwide. For further information about international editions, contact your local Microsoft Corporation office or contact Microsoft Press International directly at fax (425) 936-7329. Visit our Web site at mspress.microsoft.com.

A Quick Course® Education/Training Edition for this title is published by Online Training Solutions, Inc. (OTSI). For information about supplementary workbooks, contact OTSI at 15442 Bel-Red Road, Redmond, WA 98052, USA, 1-800-854-3344. E-mail: quickcourse@ otsiweb.com.

Authors: Joyce Cox and Christina Dudley
Acquisitions Editor: Susanne M. Forderer
Project Editor: Anne Taussig

From the publisher

Quick Course®... The name says it all.

In today's busy world, everyone seems to be looking for easier methods, faster solutions, and shortcuts to success. That's why we decided to publish the Quick Course® series.

Why Choose A Quick Course®?

When all the computer books claim to be fast, easy, and complete, how can you be sure you're getting exactly the one that will do the job for you? You can depend on Quick Course® books because they give you:

- Everything you need to do useful work, in two easy-to-tackle parts: "Learning the Basics" (for beginning users) and "Building Proficiency" (for intermediate users).

- Easy-to-follow numbered instructions and thorough explanations.

- To-the-point directions for creating professional-looking documents that can be recycled and customized with your own data.

- Numerous screen shots to help you follow along when you're not at the computer.

- Handy pointers to key terms and tasks for quick lookup and review.

- Consistent quality—the same team of people creates them all. If you like one, you'll like the others!

We at Microsoft Press are proud of our reputation for producing quality products that meet the needs of our readers. We are confident that this Quick Course® book will live up to your expectations.

Jim Brown,
Publisher

Content overview

Content details

PART ONE: LEARNING THE BASICS

PART TWO: BUILDING PROFICIENCY

PART ONE

LEARNING THE BASICS

In Part One, you learn basic techniques for working with simple Publisher documents. In Chapter 1, you begin by creating a promotional postcard, paying close attention to color schemes, text, and the various components that are common to all publications. In Chapter 2, you use a wizard to design a flyer and then learn how to work with frames and combine formatting options. Finally, in Chapter 3, you see how to make your publications stand out by adding graphics, fancy text, and other visual enhancements.

1

Creating a Simple Publication

After a brief introduction to the program, you jump right in and create your first publication. You learn the various parts of a publication, how to work with color schemes and text, and how to save and print your work. Finally, you learn how to get help and quit Publisher.

You create a promotional postcard for a business in this chapter, but you can use the same techniques to design any type of postcard, such as an appointment reminder, an event announcement, or a change of address.

Publications created and concepts covered:

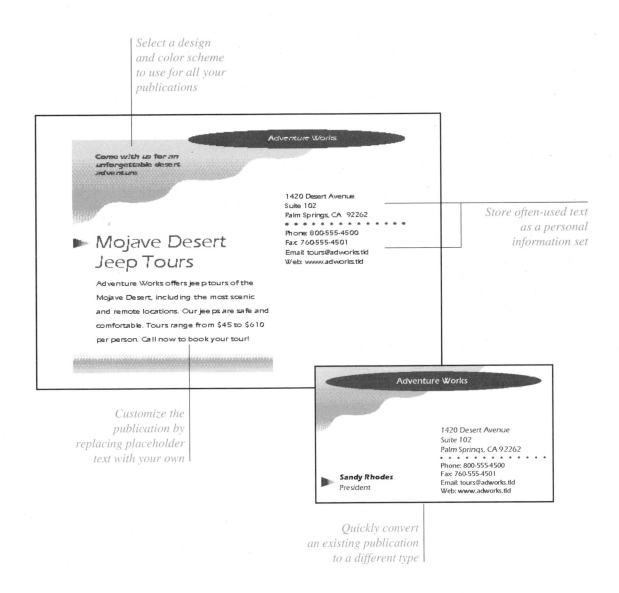

Select a design and color scheme to use for all your publications

Adventure Works

Come with us for an unforgettable desert adventure

1420 Desert Avenue
Suite 102
Palm Springs, CA 92262
Phone: 800-555-4500
Fax: 760-555-4501
Email: tours@adworks.tld
Web: www.adworks.tld

Store often-used text as a personal information set

▶ Mojave Desert Jeep Tours

Adventure Works offers jeep tours of the Mojave Desert, including the most scenic and remote locations. Our jeeps are safe and comfortable. Tours range from $45 to $610 per person. Call now to book your tour!

Customize the publication by replacing placeholder text with your own

Adventure Works

1420 Desert Avenue
Suite 102
Palm Springs, CA 92262
Phone: 800-555-4500
Fax: 760-555-4501
Email: tours@adworks.tld
Web: www.adworks.tld

▶ **Sandy Rhodes**
President

Quickly convert an existing publication to a different type

Most businesses and organizations use a variety of printed publications as promotional and informational materials. You probably have several business cards in your wallet, receive a handful of newsletters in the mail each week, and pick up the occasional flyer or two to get information about a product or service. The effectiveness of these pieces depends on their ability to catch your eye, hold your interest, and convey their message efficiently.

Suppose you are in charge of creating promotional materials for a company called Adventure Works that offers jeep tours of the Mojave Desert. How are you going to generate publications that will look attractive and get the word out about your company's services? Obviously, you could hire a professional designer to guide you and do most of the work. But suppose you don't have the budget to take this approach. You need to be able to create functional, good-looking pieces yourself. That's where a sophisticated desktop-publishing package like Microsoft Publisher 2000 comes in.

With Publisher, you can focus on the message of a publication and let the program handle many of the aesthetic details. In fact, Publisher can help with virtually every facet of creating a publication, so you can easily produce professional-quality documents. At the same time, Publisher allows you to tailor various components to your own needs and tastes, and you're never constrained by the program's ideas of what a particular publication should look like.

In this book, we focus on how to use Publisher to produce simple, yet effective publications for Adventure Works. You will easily be able to adapt these examples to your needs. Because adequate planning and a basic knowledge of good design are essential if you want your publications to have maximum impact, we weave these topics into the chapters where appropriate. By the time you have worked through this book, you'll know not only how to use Publisher but how to develop a variety of publications that accomplish your goals.

We assume that you have already installed both Microsoft Windows 95 or a later version and Microsoft Publisher 2000

Other ways to start Publisher

Instead of starting Publisher by choosing it from the Start menu, you can create a shortcut icon for Publisher on your desktop. Right-click an open area of the desktop and choose New and then Shortcut from the shortcut menu. In the Create Shortcut dialog box, click the Browse button, navigate to C:\Program Files\Microsoft Office\Office\mspub, and then click Next. Type a name for the shortcut icon and click Finish. For maximum efficiency, you can start Publisher and then open a recently used publication by choosing the publication from the Documents submenu of the Start menu, where Windows stores the names of up to 15 of the most recently opened files. If you are using Microsoft Office 2000, you can also choose Open Office Document from the top of the Start menu and navigate to the folder in which the document you want to open is stored. To start Publisher and open a new publication, you can choose New Office Document from the top of the Start menu and then double-click the Blank Publication icon. When Publisher starts, you see the Catalog dialog box as usual.

on your computer. We also assume that you've worked with Windows before and that you know how to start programs, move windows, choose commands from menus, highlight text, and so on. If you are a new Windows user, we suggest you take a look at *Quick Course® in Microsoft Windows*, which will help you come up to speed.

It's time to get started, so let's fire up Publisher:

1. Click the Start button at the left end of the Windows taskbar, choose Programs, and then choose Microsoft Publisher from the Programs submenu. The Publisher window opens, immediately followed by this Catalog dialog box:

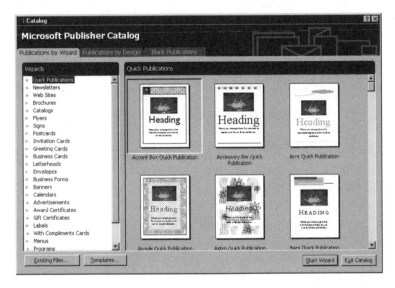

Starting Publisher

You see this dialog box every time you start Publisher. As you can see, it has three tabs. The Publications By Wizard tab, which is currently displayed, lists in its left pane the wizards available to help you create various types of publications, such as newsletters, flyers, and business cards. Selecting a type from the Wizards list in the left pane displays in the window's right pane miniature pictures of the designs available for that type of publication. These designs are consistent from one type to another, so you can create a collection of publications that have the same overall look.

Wizards

Wizard's work in the same basic way, regardless of the application or the task. Each wizard asks a series of questions, and you provide answers by typing in an edit box or selecting from various options. You can move from question to question by clicking the Next button, and you can also move back to an earlier question by clicking the Back button. To tell the wizard to complete the task using the information you have provided, click the Finish button.

2. Click the Publications By Design tab. Now the left pane of the dialog box lists the available designs. Selecting a design from the list displays in the right pane miniature pictures of the types of publications you can create with that design.

3. Click the Blank Publications tab. Again, the dialog box changes to display the types of blank publications you can create from scratch.

Using a Wizard to Create a Publication

Suppose you have decided to create an informational post-card that will be displayed in the lobbies of local hotels. You want it to briefly describe the Adventure Works tours and their price ranges. You are using Publisher for the first time, and you want to take advantage of all the help you can get. For your first publication, you're going to let one of Publisher's wizards be your guide. Wizards ask a few questions to get the ball rolling, and then you can type in your own text and cus-tomize the publication by adding, subtracting, or changing various elements. For now, though, you want to keep cus-tomization to a minimum while you get used to the program. Follow these steps to see how to use one of Publisher's wiz-ards to quickly create a professional-looking publication with very little fuss:

1. Click the Publications By Wizard tab in the Catalog dialog box, and click Postcards once in the Wizards list in the left pane. The right pane now displays the available postcard types, as shown on the facing page.

Initial capital letters

Sometimes the capitalization of the option names we use doesn't ex-actly match what's on the screen. We capitalize the first letter of every word to set these words off in a sentence. For example, in the above steps we tell you to click the Publications By Design tab when the tab name on the screen is Publications by Design.

Clicking, double-clicking, and right-clicking

For beginner users, here's a quick recap of mouse terminology. For right-handed users, the left mouse button is the primary button, and the right mouse button is the secondary button. If you are left-handed and have switched the action of the mouse buttons, the right button is the primary button, and the left button is the secondary button. *Clicking* means press-ing and releasing the primary mouse button once. *Double-clicking* means pressing and releasing the primary mouse button twice in rapid succes-sion. *Right-clicking* means pressing and releasing the secondary mouse button once.

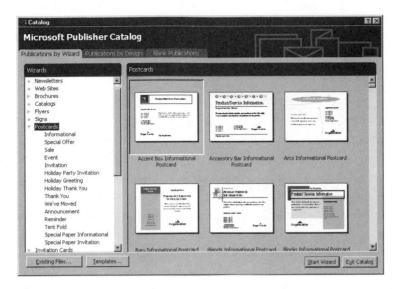

2. Click Event in the list of postcard types to display pictures of the available event postcard designs in the right pane.

Selecting a publication type

3. Now click Informational at the top of the list in the left pane to display pictures of the available informational postcard designs in the right pane.

4. Next use the right pane's scroll bar to move down the list until you see the Tilt Informational Postcard. (See the tip below if you need a refresher on how to use scroll bars.) Then if necessary, click the Tilt Informational Postcard once to select it. (It will be surrounded by a box that makes it look "pressed.")

Using scroll bars

Publisher's window is often not big enough to display all of its contents. To bring out-of-sight information into view, you can use the scroll bars. Clicking the arrow at the end of a scroll bar moves the window's contents a small distance in the direction of the arrow. Clicking on either side of the scroll box in the scroll bar moves the contents one windowful. The position of the scroll box in relation to the scroll bar indicates the position of the window in relation to its contents. For example, if the scroll box is at the top of the vertical scroll bar, you are viewing the top of the page. You can drag the scroll box to see a specific part of the page.

5. Click the Start Wizard button at the bottom of the dialog box. Publisher closes the dialog box, starts the wizard, and displays the dialog box shown here:

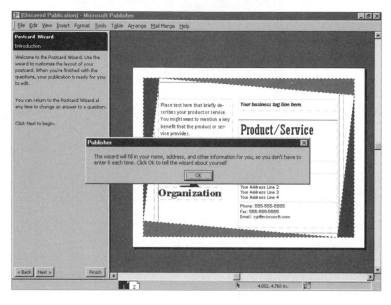

Personal information set →

6. Click OK to move to this dialog box, where you can store information about yourself and your organization in a *personal information set*:

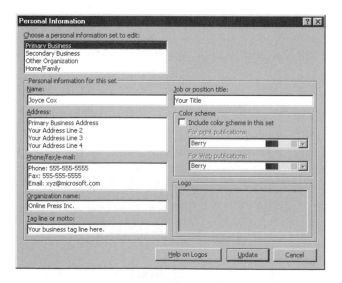

7. With Primary Business selected, replace the entry in the Name edit box with *Sandy Rhodes*. Then replace the entry in the Job Or Position Title edit box with *President*.

8. Fill in the remaining boxes with the information shown here:

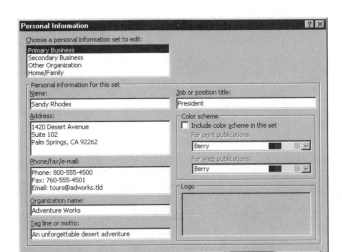

9. You want all the publications you create for Adventure Works to have the same color scheme, so click the Include Color Scheme In This Set check box to turn it on. Then click the arrow to the right of the For Print Publications box and select Desert from the drop-down list. Then select Desert as the For Web Publications setting.

10. Click the Update button to close the Personal Information dialog box and update your personal information set.

Now you're ready to work with the Postcard Wizard to create your first publication. Follow these steps:

1. Read the information in the wizard's pane on the left side of the window, and click Next at the bottom of the pane. The wizard's pane changes to display a list of color schemes.

2. Click some of the color schemes and notice their effect on the postcard in the right pane. When you are ready, reselect Desert, and then click Next. The wizard's pane changes again to allow you to select either a quarter-page or half-page postcard.

3. You want the postcard to be a quarter page, so leave that option selected and click Next. The wizard's pane now displays a list of options for the back of the postcard.

Other personal information sets

Publisher can maintain up to four personal information sets: Primary Business, Secondary Business, Other Organization, and Home/Family. For each set, Publisher stores the eight items of information shown in the adjacent dialog box. By default, Publisher uses the Primary Business set when you create publications. To apply a different set to a publication, choose Personal Information from the Edit menu, select a set from the list box at the top of the Personal Information dialog box, review the information in all the edit boxes, and click Update. (You also use this command to change an item of information.) To insert a particular item from the active personal information set in a publication, choose Personal Information and then the desired item from the Insert menu. Publisher inserts the selected item in the publication in its own text frame. You can then format the text and frame as needed. (We discuss formatting text and working with frames in Chapter 2.) Once an item has been inserted in a publication, you can add to it or delete parts of it without affecting the way it is stored in the personal information set.

4. You want to be able to mail these postcards, so with Only Address selected, click Next.

5. Check that One In The Center Of The Page is selected, and click Next.

6. You've already filled in the information for the Primary Business personal information set, so click Finish. Your screen now looks like this:

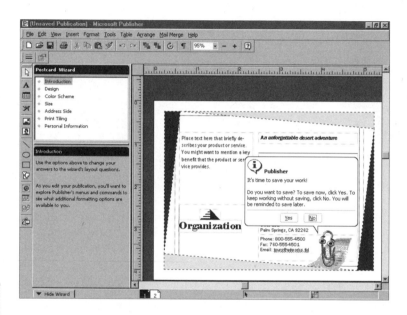

7. As you can see, the Office Assistant has popped up to remind you to save your work. Click No for now. (We discuss the Office Assistant on page 32. Other than responding to messages by clicking an option, you can ignore it for now. If your Office Assistant is hidden or turned off, you see the messages in a dialog box instead of as shown above.)

8. Publisher has left the wizard open so that you can modify the postcard if necessary. Click the Hide Wizard button below the wizard's pane to give the postcard more space on the screen.

9. Another way to give the postcard more space is to hide the Windows taskbar, as we've done. To hide your taskbar, right-click a blank area of the taskbar, choose Properties, select the AutoHide option, and click OK. Your screen now looks as shown on the facing page.

Objects toolbar   *Menu bar*   *Title bar*

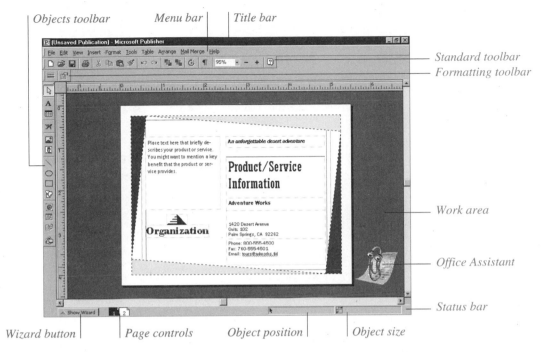

Standard toolbar

Formatting toolbar

Work area

Office Assistant

Status bar

Wizard button   *Page controls*   *Object position*   *Object size*

Because the Hide Wizard button is now the Show Wizard button, you can easily display the wizard again at any time.

Taking up most of the work area of the Microsoft Publisher window is your new postcard, parts of which have been customized with the information from your personal information set. Like most Windows applications, the Publisher window includes the familiar title bar at the top and a status bar at the bottom. You also see a menu bar and toolbars, which you use to give Publisher instructions. Although the menu bar and toolbars look the same as those in all Windows applications, they work a little differently, so we'll take a moment to explore them here.

You use standard Windows techniques to choose a command from a menu or submenu and to work with dialog boxes. However, Publisher 2000 goes beyond the basic Windows procedure for choosing commands by determining which commands you are most likely to use and then adjusting the display of commands on each menu to reflect how you use

Shortcut menus

For efficiency, the commands you are likely to use with a particular object in a publication (such as a text frame) or in the publication window (such as a toolbar) are grouped together on special menus called *shortcut menus*. You can display an object's shortcut menu by pointing to the object and clicking the right mouse button. (This action is known as *right-clicking*; see the tip on page 6.)

the program. As a quick example, let's take a look at the View menu:

Short menus

1. Click *View* on the menu bar to drop down the View menu. The two arrows at the bottom of the menu indicate that one or more commands are hidden because they are not the ones most people use most of the time.

Expanded menus

2. Continue pointing to the word *View*. The two arrows disappear and the menu expands to display more commands, like this:

(You can also click the two arrows to make hidden commands appear.) The status of a less frequently used command is indicated by a lighter shade of gray. If you choose one of the light gray commands, in the future it will appear in the same color as other commands and will no longer be hidden.

Turning off the rulers

3. Choose the Rulers command. The rulers above and to the left of the work area disappear.

4. Drop down the View menu and notice that the Rulers command now appears on the short menu.

5. Move the pointer along the menu bar, pausing to drop down each menu in turn. Notice that once one menu is expanded, they all are.

Turning off the Office Assistant

6. When you reach the Help menu, choose Hide The Office Assistant to temporarily turn off the Office Assistant.

Another way to give Publisher an instruction is by clicking a button on a *toolbar*. This is the equivalent of choosing the corresponding command from a menu and if necessary, clicking

OK to accept all the default settings in the command's dialog box. By default, Publisher arranges its buttons on three toolbars: the Standard and Formatting toolbars above the work area, and the Objects toolbar down the left side of the screen. The Standard and Objects toolbars are static, meaning that they display the same buttons no matter what task you are carrying out. The Formatting toolbar changes depending on what element of your publication is selected. Try this:

1. First point to each button on the Formatting toolbar. Publisher's *ScreenTips* feature displays a box with the button's name. ◄ ScreenTips

2. Click anywhere in the words *Adventure Works*. Publisher surrounds the frame that contains the words with small black squares called *handles* to indicate that the frame is selected. ◄ Selection handles
The Formatting toolbar changes to look like this:

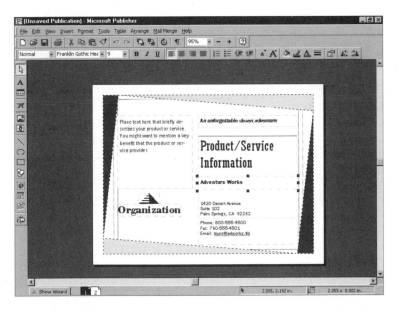

3. Now click the pyramid graphic above the word *Organization*. The Formatting toolbar changes again.

The menu bar and each toolbar has a *move handle* at its left or ◄ Move handles
top end. You can drag this handle to change the location of the toolbar on the screen. Follow the steps on the next page to do some exploring.

Floating toolbars ────────────►

1. Point to the Formatting toolbar's move handle. When the pointer changes to a four-headed arrow, drag it down over the work area. It becomes a "floating" toolbar, like the one here:

Docking toolbars ──────────────►

2. Double-click the toolbar's title bar to "dock" it at the top of the work area again.

Displaying toolbars ────────────►
on the same row

3. Now drag the toolbar's move handle up and to the right to display the Formatting toolbar on the same row as the Standard toolbar, as shown here:

Standard toolbar | *Move handle* | *Formatting toolbar*

When a graphic is selected, there's room on the toolbar row to display the entire Formatting toolbar.

4. Click *Adventure Works*. The Formatting toolbar changes to show the buttons pertaining to the new selection. The toolbar row no longer has room to display both the Standard and Formatting toolbars in their entirety, so Publisher hides the buttons on each toolbar that you are less likely to use and adds a More Buttons button at the right end of each toolbar so that you can access the hidden buttons, like this:

The More Buttons button ────────►

More Buttons buttons

5. Suppose you want to see more of the Formatting toolbar's buttons and don't mind seeing fewer of the Standard toolbar's buttons. Drag the Formatting toolbar's move handle to the left as far as you can.

Docking elsewhere

You can dock a toolbar along any of the four sides of the program window simply by dragging it there. (Drag a docked toolbar by its move handle or a floating toolbar by its title bar.) If you drag a docked toolbar over the work area and double-click the floating toolbar's title bar to redock it, the toolbar automatically returns to its previous docked location.

6. Click the Standard toolbar's More Buttons button to see this palette of all the hidden buttons on that toolbar:

7. Because the postcard is small enough to fit in the work area, drag the Formatting toolbar back to its original location below the Standard toolbar so that you can see all the buttons on both bars.

You'll work extensively with the buttons on all three toolbars as you work your way through this book. For now, let's save the publication on your screen.

Saving a Publication

To save a new publication, you can click the Save button on the Standard toolbar or choose Save As from the File menu. Publisher then displays a dialog box in which you specify the publication's name. Follow these steps:

The Save button

1. Choose Save As from the File menu. Publisher displays the Save As dialog box:

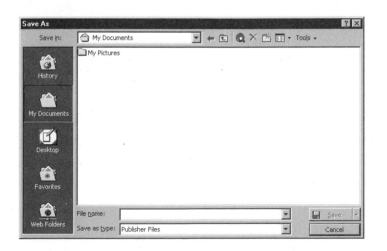

Personalized menus

As you have noticed, Publisher's menus adjust themselves to the way that you work, making more commands available as you use them. Commands that you don't use are hidden so they don't get in the way. Therefore, your menus may not look exactly like ours, and occasionally, we may tell you to choose a command that is not visible. When this happens, don't panic. Simply pull down the menu and wait until it expands so that all its commands are displayed.

2. With the insertion point in the File Name edit box, type *Postcard.*

3. Be sure the My Documents folder appears in the Save In box and, leaving the other settings in the dialog box as they are, click Save. When you return to the publication, notice that Postcard has replaced Unsaved Publication in the title bar.

Saving an existing publication →

From now on, you can simply click the Save button or choose the Save command any time you want to save changes to this file. Because Publisher knows the name of the file, it over-writes the previous version with the new version. If you want to save your changes but preserve the previous version, you can assign a different name to the new version by choosing the Save As command from the File menu, entering the new name in the File Name edit box, and clicking Save.

As you have seen, Publisher also periodically reminds you to save your work. (When the Office Assistant is turned off, Publisher displays these reminders in a message box.) To save the file, click Yes. To wait and save later, simply click No. (See the tip below for more information.)

Saving options

By default, a publication is saved with the Publisher Files format and a template is saved with the Publisher Templates format (see page 127). To save a file with a different format, click the arrow to the right of the Save As Type edit box in the Save As dialog box, and select the format you need from the drop-down list. If you want to keep a backup copy of your work, click the arrow to the right of the Save button (in the Save As dialog box), and then select Save With Backup from the drop-down list. The backup file will be called *Backup Of Filename* and saved in the same folder.

Saving in another folder

To store the file in a folder different from the one in the Save In box, click the arrow to the right of the Save In box, and use the drop-down list to find the folder in which you want the file saved. Double-click that folder and then click Save. You can also use the icons on the shortcuts bar along the left side of the Save As dialog box to quickly move to common folders and recent files. To create a folder, click the Create New Folder button before you save the file. To change the default folder from My Documents, choose Options from the Tools menu, and in the File Locations section, click the Modify button.

Save reminders

By default, Publisher reminds you every 15 minutes to save the publication you are working on. You can save your work simply by clicking Yes. If you want to change the frequency of the reminders or turn off the feature altogether, choose Options from the Tools menu and click the User Assistance tab. You can change the setting in the Minutes Between Reminders box to see the reminders more or less frequently. You can click the Remind To Save Publication check box to remove the check mark, which turns the feature off. Click OK to implement your changes.

Moving Around a Publication

You need to know how to move around a publication for two reasons: so that you can view parts of a publication that do not fit in the window, and so that you can edit its text.

If a page of a publication is bigger than the window, you can bring hidden parts into view by using the scroll bars (see the tip on page 7). To display a different page of a publication, you can use the page controls in the status bar. Let's try out these controls now:

1. Click the page labeled 2 on the status bar. Publisher displays page 2 of the publication, which, as you can see here, is the back of the postcard:

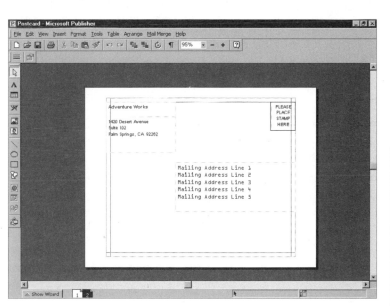

Moving to a different page

2. Now choose Go To Page from the View menu to display the dialog box shown below. (You can also press Ctrl+G to open this dialog box.)

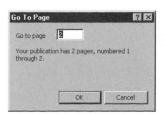

Keyboard shortcuts

Publisher provides many keyboard shortcuts for working with publications. If a command has a shortcut, it is displayed to the right of the command on the menu. Shortcuts are also available for moving around, applying formatting, and other common tasks. Unfortunately, the list is too lengthy to reproduce here. If you have worked with Microsoft Word and know that program's keyboard shortcuts, you can use many of them in Publisher. If you are not familiar with these shortcuts, look up *keyboard* and then *use shortcuts* in Publisher's Help feature. (We discuss how to get help on page 32.)

3. Replace the 2 in the edit box with *1*, and click OK to return to page 1 of the publication. (This command is more useful when your publication has several pages.)

Zooming In and Out

In addition to scrolling around a large page and moving to different pages of a multi-page publication, you will also want to zoom in for a closer look at a particular element or zoom out to get an overview of an entire page. With Publisher, you can zoom in and out in several ways. Before you start working on the text of the postcard, let's experiment with zooming:

The Zoom box

1. Click the arrow to the right of the Zoom box on the Standard toolbar to display a drop-down list of standard zoom percentages. Also included in the list is the Whole Page option, which zooms to the size that allows you to view the entire page, and the Page Width option, which expands the publication to fill the work area. If you select an object on the page, Publisher adds a Selected Objects option, which zooms the window to the percentage that allows full viewing of the object.

2. Click 200% to zoom in on the postcard like this:

Another zooming option

When you want to quickly switch between the current view and the actual size view (100%), you can press the F9 key.

3. Next choose Zoom from the View menu to display the same list as a submenu, and then go ahead and return the zoom percentage to 100%.

4. To zoom out to the next lowest increment, click the Zoom Out button on the Standard toolbar. Publisher switches the view to 75%.

The Zoom Out button

The Zoom In button

5. Click the Zoom In button to return to 100%.

Identifying Parts of a Publication

As you move the mouse pointer over the postcard now on your screen, you may notice ScreenTips boxes popping up to identify its different parts. Try this:

1. Move the pointer over the words *Adventure Works* and pause for a moment. Publisher displays a pop-up box with the description *Organization Name Text Frame*.

2. Now move the pointer over the address below and pause. The ScreenTips box identifies this part of the postcard as the *Address Text Frame*.

3. We'll refer to these ScreenTips identifiers in our instructions, so if you don't see the pop-up boxes, choose Toolbars and then Options from the View menu to display the dialog box shown below:

Turning on ScreenTips

4. Make sure your settings are the same as those you see here and click OK.

If you still have trouble getting the ScreenTips to appear, be patient and be sure to pause over the item.

Stories ————————————▶

Placeholders ————————————▶

Tippages ————————————▶

The Ungroup Objects button ————————————▶

Working with Text

Unlike text in a word processing program, text displayed in the Publisher window must be contained in a text frame. Publisher refers to the text in a frame as a *story*. We discuss working with frames in Chapter 2. For now, we'll just show you how to handle the text inside the postcard's existing frames. As you can see, some of the postcard's frames contain *placeholders*, meaning that Publisher has used dummy text to show you what to place where. You need to select the placeholders and replace them with your own words. The simplest way to learn how to select text is to actually do it, so let's get going:

1. Click anywhere in the Product/Service Information placeholder. (If you see a "bubble" telling you that you can press Ctrl+A to select all the text in a story, press Esc to close it. See the tip below for information about this type of helpful hint, which is called a *tippage*.) Publisher changes all the text in the frame to white on black (called *highlighting*) to ensure that it is replaced by whatever you type. Publisher also displays an Ungroup Objects button below the selected frame. Although you can't see it very well, the frame has a line above it, and the frame and line have been grouped so that if you move, size, or delete one, the other will be moved, sized, or deleted as well. (We talk more about lines on page 53 and about grouping objects on page 89.)

Tippages

Tippages are yellow "bubbles" that occasionally pop up to offer advice on more efficient ways to carry out specific tasks. To remove a tippage from the screen, click it or press Esc. If you find this feature a nuisance, you can turn it off. Choose Options from the Tools menu, click the User Assistance tab, deselect the Show Tippages check box, and click OK. To reset tippages so that ones you have seen before reappear under similar circumstances, click the Reset Tips button.

2. With the text selected, type *Mojave Desert Jeep Toors* and press the Spacebar. (Be sure to misspell *Tours*.) Publisher underlines the misspelling with a red, wavy line to draw the error to your attention. We'll show you how to correct this mistake on page 27, but for now, simply ignore it.

3. Click anywhere in the *Place text here* placeholder to select both the text and the frame, and then type the following paragraph (including the spelling errors in bold):

*Adventure Works offers jeep **toors** of the Mojave Desert, including the most remote and **seanic** locations. Tours range from $45 to $610 per person. Our jeeps are safe and **comfortable**. Call now to book **you're** tour!*

4. You may have already responded to Publisher's prompting and saved your work, but to be on the cautious side, click the Save button on the Standard toolbar.

Now let's adjust some of the information Publisher has drawn from your personal information set:

1. Double-click the word *An* in the tag-line frame in the top right corner to select the word and the following space. Then type *Come with **use** for an.* (If you have trouble seeing the text, use one of the zooming techniques described on page 18 to change the zoom magnification.) As the words you type fill the frame, Publisher automatically adjusts the text size to make it fit. Why? Because a formatting feature called *automatic copy-fitting* (see the tip on page 43) has been applied to this frame so that the tag line will always be a single line.

◄——— Automatic copyfitting

2. To add a new line of text to the phone/fax/e-mail text frame in the bottom right corner, click an insertion point at the end of the e-mail address and press Enter. Then type *Web: www.adworks.tld.* Here are the results:

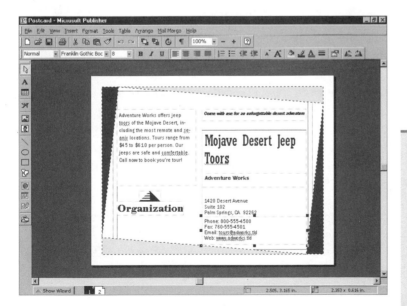

Whole word selection

By default, Publisher selects whole words. For example, if you start a selection in the middle of a word and then drag beyond the last character, Publisher selects the entire word. You can tell Publisher to select only the characters you drag across by choosing Options from the Tools menu and clicking the Edit tab. Next click the When Selecting Automatically Select Entire Word check box to deselect it and click OK.

Deleting Text

Sometimes you will want to delete a placeholder without replacing it with anything. (Always delete placeholders; otherwise, they appear just as they are when you print the final publication.) When you want to delete only the text in a frame, you can select the text and press the Delete key. If you want to delete a frame as well as the text it contains, you must use another method. To demonstrate, let's delete the Logo placeholder on the left side of the postcard:

Deleting extraneous text

Deleting frames

1. Click the word *Organization* in the Logo placeholder to select it. (Because a wizard is associated with the logo, a Wizard button appears below the frame. You'll develop a logo using this wizard in Chapter 3.)

2. With the logo frame selected, drop down the Edit menu, wait for it to expand, and then choose Delete Object. The logo disappears.

3. Click the Save button to save Postcard.

Moving and Copying Text

Like most Windows applications, Publisher provides two methods for moving text. The first method involves cutting and pasting, which is useful for moving text from one page to another or even from one publication to another. The second method involves dragging and dropping, which is useful for moving text to a different location on the same page. Similarly, two methods are provided for copying text. (You'll try your hand at copying and pasting from one publication to another in Chapter 2.) Let's experiment:

Using Word to edit text

Publisher 2000 is very similar to Microsoft Word in its text editing techniques and capabilities. However, if you installed Publisher as part of the Microsoft Office 2000 suite, then you have Word 2000 installed on your computer, and you can use that program to edit your text. This ability to move text between the two programs is handy for longer publications or if you simply prefer to use Word for text editing. To edit text in Word, select the text frame that contains the text you want to edit, right-click the frame and choose Change Text and then Edit Story In Microsoft Word from the shortcut menu. Word starts and displays the text in a document window. When you finish editing the text, you can exit Word and update the Publisher file by choosing the Close & Return command from Word's File menu.

1. Select the sentence that begins *Our jeeps* by holding down the left mouse button while you drag through the sentence. Or you can click an insertion point to the left of the *O*, hold down the Shift key, and press the Arrow keys until the sentence is highlighted.

2. Click the Cut button. Publisher removes the text from the publication and stores it in a temporary storage place called the *Clipboard* in your computer's memory. If you want to copy text instead of moving it, click the Copy button.

The Cut button

The Copy button

3. Click an insertion point to the left of *T* in *Tours* and then click the Paste button. Publisher inserts the cut text, following it with a space.

The Paste button

4. Next double-click the word *remote* to select it and click the Cut button.

5. Click an insertion point to the left of the *s* in *seanic* and click the Paste button.

Now try dragging and dropping:

1. Double-click the word *seanic* and point to the selection. (The word *DRAG* appears below the pointer.)

Drag-and-drop editing

2. Hold down the left mouse button, drag the selection to the left of *a* in *and*, and then release the button. (The word *MOVE* appears below the pointer as you drag.) Publisher moves the word to its new location, adjusting the spaces appropriately. The words *remote* and *seanic* have now switched places.

The Clipboard

The Clipboard temporarily stores cut or copied data from all Windows applications. Because the Clipboard is a temporary storage place, turning off your computer erases any information stored there. You can use the Clipboard to transfer data from one file to another in the same application or from one application to another. Each item you cut or copy overwrites the previous item. To preserve information that's already on the Clipboard, you can use drag-and-drop techniques, which don't use this temporary storage area.

Moving and copying with the keyboard

To use the keyboard to cut text, select the text and press Ctrl+X. Then to paste it, click an insertion point and press Ctrl+V. To copy text instead of moving it, follow the same procedure but use Ctrl+C instead of Ctrl+X.

To copy text using drag-and-drop, hold down the Ctrl key while dragging the selection.

Undoing and Redoing Commands

For those occasions when you make a mistake or have second thoughts about a change you have made, Publisher provides a safety net: the Undo command. Try this:

The Undo button

The Redo button

1. You're not sure you like the words in their new order, so click the Undo button to reverse the drag operation from the previous steps.

2. Change your mind again, and click the Redo button to drag *seanic* back before *and*. Then click a blank area of the screen. With all the text in place, the postcard now looks like this:

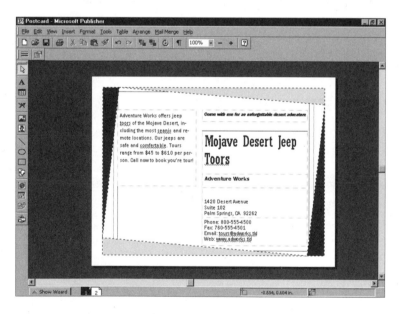

Using a Wizard to Make Design Changes

You've seen how to simplify the task of creating a publication by using one of Publisher's wizards. Obviously, adding text is easier when the text frames for all the elements are already in place. But what if you decide you don't like the design or color scheme you chose? Do you have to start all over again?

Using AutoCorrect

Publisher's AutoCorrect feature corrects simple typos as you enter text in a frame. For example, if you type *teh*, AutoCorrect replaces it with *the*. AutoCorrect also corrects two initial capital letters, such as *ADventure*, and capitalizes the names of days. To include your own commonly misspelled entries in Auto-Correct, choose AutoCorrect from the Tools menu. When the AutoCorrect dialog box appears, type the misspelling in the Replace edit box, type the correct spelling in the With edit box, and click Add. AutoCorrect adds the new entry to its list of common misspellings. To delete entries from AutoCorrect's list, select the entry and click the Delete button. To turn the AutoCorrect feature off, deselect the Replace Text As You Type check box in the AutoCorrect dialog box.

No. You can simply call on the wizard to make these sorts of changes.

Changing the Basic Design

Suppose you've decided that the Tilt design doesn't quite fit the image you want for Adventure Works. Let's open the wizard again and look for something more appropriate:

1. With the postcard still displayed on your screen, click the Show Wizard button at the left end of the status bar at the bottom of the window. The wizard's pane opens, with an outline of the process by which it creates a publication displayed at the top and the instructions for the step selected in the process displayed at the bottom, as shown here:

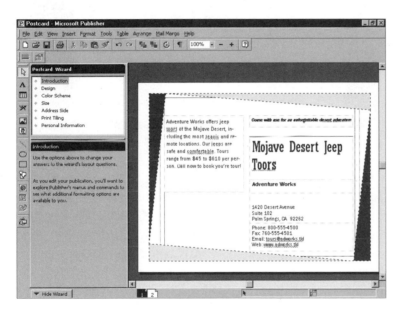

Displaying the publication's wizard

2. Click Design in the outline to display the wizard's instructions for that step. (Notice that you can change the postcard's type as well as its design.)

3. If necessary, scroll the list upward so that you can see all the designs that are available for the Informational type. Click the Blocks design and note the results in the pane on the right.

Resetting designs

If you don't like some of the changes you have made to your Publisher-designed work, you can restore the original settings. First display the wizard for the open publication and click the Design step in the top part of the wizard's pane to display the list of available designs in the bottom part of the pane. Then with the current design selected, click the Reset Design button. Publisher displays the Reset Design dialog box where you can click check boxes to reset the original formatting, restore deleted objects, and reestablish the original layout. You can also remove objects and pages you have added and restore text and pictures you have changed. Click OK to reverse the specified design changes.

4. This design doesn't really fit the tone you want for a company providing a service to tourists, so experiment with some of the other design templates, and then finish by selecting Waves.

5. Click the Hide Wizard button to display the postcard with its new design, as shown here:

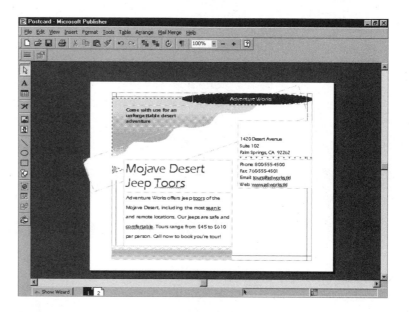

Changing the Color Scheme

If you are going to print your publication in color, you need to carefully consider its color scheme. Choosing colors that are appropriate for the message you want to send is very important. If you understand how colors work together and their effects on your audience, you will probably have no trouble devising your own color schemes. The rest of us can be thankful that Publisher provides a number of preset color schemes to choose from.

Although the Desert color scheme seemed appropriate when you chose it earlier, the brown doesn't suit a tourist activity. Let's find a more sophisticated scheme:

1. Click the Show Wizard button to redisplay the wizard's pane, and then click Color Scheme in the top pane.

2. Scroll through the list and select any color schemes that catch your eye, noting their effects on the postcard in the pane on the right. When you finish experimenting, click Tropics.

3. Click the Hide Wizard button to close the wizard and get a better look at the postcard's new colors. This scheme includes colors you might find in the desert but is more vibrant.

4. Save your work.

Checking Spelling

Now that you have entered the postcard's text and finalized its design and color scheme, you're ready to print, right? Not quite. Before printing any publication, you should always check it for spelling and other errors. As you added the text, you deliberately included a few misspellings, and Publisher flagged most of them with red, wavy underlines. This feature, called *automatic spell-checking*, alerts you to errors as you work. Let's fix one of the misspelled words now:

Automatic spell-checking

1. Point to the word *comfortable* in the bottom left corner and right-click it. Publisher checks the underlined word against its built-in dictionary and displays this shortcut menu:

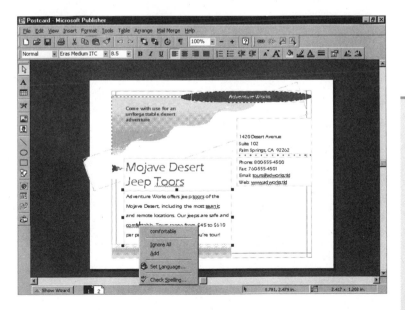

Spelling options

As you have seen, Publisher flags any misspellings you type with the red, wavy underlines. It also flags duplicate words, such as *the the*, and words in all uppercase letters. If you don't want Publisher to flag these items, choose Spelling and then Spelling Options from the Tools menu to display the Spelling Options dialog box. Then select or deselect the appropriate options and click OK.

At the top of the shortcut menu, Publisher displays any words in its dictionary that resemble the misspelled word. You can replace the underlined word with one of Publisher's suggestions, ignore the misspelling, add the underlined word to Publisher's dictionary so that the program will recognize the word in the future, set the default language used, or open the Check Spelling dialog box for more options.

2. Choose *comfortable* from the shortcut menu to replace the word with its correct spelling.

You can also check the spelling of an entire publication. Follow these steps:

Spell-checking an entire publication

1. Click an insertion point in the title text frame (the one that begins *Mojave Desert*) and choose Spelling and then Check Spelling from the Tools menu. Publisher checks each word in the selected text frame against its built-in dictionary, starting with the word containing the insertion point. When it finds a word that is not in its dictionary, Publisher highlights the word and displays this Check Spelling dialog box:

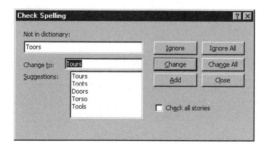

Publisher's dictionaries

Publisher checks your spelling by comparing each word in the publication with those in both its built-in dictionary and the Custom.dic supplemental dictionary. You cannot change the built-in dictionary, but you can add the words you use often to Custom.dic by clicking the Add button in the Check Spelling dialog box.

Possible alternatives for *Toors* appear in the Suggestions list, with the closest match to the unrecognized word displayed in the Change To edit box. (Notice that Publisher's suggestions have the same capitalization as the word identified as a misspelling.)

2. Before correcting the current error, click the Check All Stories check box at the bottom of the dialog box so that Publisher will spell-check all the words in the postcard, not just those in the selected frame.

3. To correct the current misspelling, check that *Tours* appears in the Change To box (click it in the Suggestions list if it doesn't.) Then click Change All to correct all occurrences of this misspelling.

4. If Publisher stops at *toors*, click Change All again.

5. Publisher stops at *seanic*. Select *scenic* in the suggestions list and click Change All.

6. The next problem Publisher identifies is the e-mail address for Adventure Works. Although this address is not in either of Publisher's dictionaries (see the tip on the facing page), it is correct, so click Add to add the address to Publisher's supplemental dictionary.

Adding words to the dictionary

7. Click Add again when Publisher stops on the Web address.

8. When Publisher reaches the end of the publication, it closes the Check Spelling dialog box and displays a message stating that the spelling check is complete. Click OK to return to the postcard.

9. Save the publication.

10. You can't rely on Publisher's spelling checker to identify every error in your publications, because errors of syntax or improper word usage can easily slip by. The postcard contains two errors of this type. Read through all the text, correct the errors when you find them, and save the postcard again.

Proofreading

Printing Publications

Once you have created and edited a publication, you will most likely want to print it. If you can print from any other Windows application, you should have no trouble printing from Publisher. Follow these steps:

1. Choose Print from the File menu to display the dialog box shown on the following page.

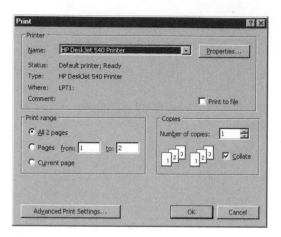

The Print button

To print the entire postcard with all the default settings in this dialog box, you can simply click the Print button on the Standard toolbar. If you want to change any of the settings—for example, if you want to print more than one copy or change which printer Publisher will use—you need to choose the Print command.

2. In the Copies section of the Print dialog box, replace the default 1 in the Number Of Copies edit box with *2* and then click OK to send the file to the printer. The postcard should look like the one shown on page 3.

For more information about some of the other printing options, see the adjacent tip or check Publisher's Help feature (see page 32).

Using Existing Information in a New Publication

Before we discuss getting help from Publisher and quitting the program, we want to show you how to quickly create another publication using the information you entered for the postcard. Let's design a business card for Adventure Works:

1. Save the postcard and then choose Close from the File menu to close the Postcard file.

2. Choose New from the File menu to display the Catalog dialog box shown earlier on page 5.

More print specifications

If you don't want Publisher to collate multiple copies of multi-page publications, click the Collate check box to deselect it. To print only the page containing the insertion point, click the Current Page option. To print selected pages, click the Pages option and then enter the page numbers (for example, enter *2-4* for pages 2, 3, and 4; and enter *2,4* for pages 2 and 4 only). Click the Print To File check box to "print" an image of the publication to a file on disk. Clicking Properties displays a tabbed dialog box with still more printing options, including the ability to switch the page orientation between Portrait (vertical) and Landscape (horizontal).

3. On the Publications By Wizard tab, click Business Cards, scroll to the Waves Business Card in the right pane, select it, and then click Start Wizard.

4. Click Next in the left pane, select Tropics as the color scheme, and click Next again.

5. Click Next to accept the default Landscape orientation, select No to remove the Logo placeholder, and click Next again.

6. With One In The Center Of The Page selected as the printing option, click Finish. Then click the Hide Wizard button. Notice that Publisher has already entered the name, title, company name, address, and phone information that you provided for your personal information set on page 9.

7. Choose Save As from the File menu and save the file in the My Documents folder with the name *Business Card*.

   You will notice that the Web address does not show up in the phone/fax/e-mail text frame because you entered it manually in the postcard. You need to enter it here, too, like this:

1. Click an insertion point at the right end of the e-mail information and press Enter to add a new line. Publisher displays the Text In Overflow indicator at the bottom of the frame to warn you that not all of the frame's text will fit in the frame. (Publisher places any extra text in a hidden place called the *overflow area*.)

The Text In Overflow indicator

2. To quickly adjust the text size so that there is room for the Web address, press Ctrl+A to select the frame's "story," click the arrow to the right of the Font Size box to display a dropdown list of sizes, and select 7. Publisher adjusts the font size, and there is now enough room in the frame for another line.

The Font Size box

3. Press End to move to the end of the selection and type *Web: www.adworks.tld*. The business card now looks like the one shown on the next page.

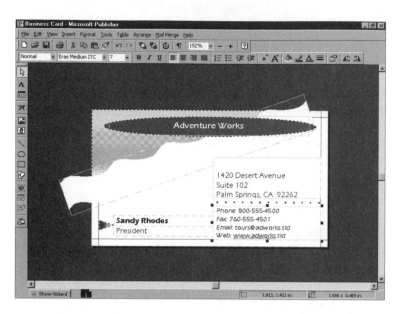

4. Click the Print button to print the business card and then save the publication.

Getting Help

This tour of Publisher has covered a lot of ground in just a few pages, and you might be wondering how you will manage to retain it all. Don't worry. If you forget how to carry out a particular task, help is never far away. You've already seen how the ScreenTips feature can jog your memory about the functions of the toolbar buttons and help you figure out the parts of a publication. And you may have noticed that the dialog boxes contain a Help button (the ? in the top right corner), which you can click to get information about their options. You may have also seen some tippages appear with brief pointers (see the tip on page 20). Here, you'll look at some ways to get information using the Office Assistant. Follow these steps:

The Microsoft Publisher Help button

1. On the Standard toolbar, click the Microsoft Publisher Help button to display the Office Assistant and a message box that asks what you want to do, as shown on the facing page. (The Office Assistant's options reflect the task you most recently completed or tried to complete.)

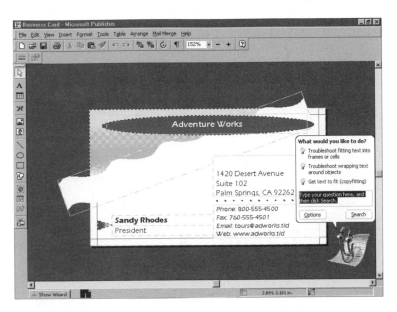

2. Type *Print a publication?* and click Search. The Office Assistant displays topics that might answer your question, like this:

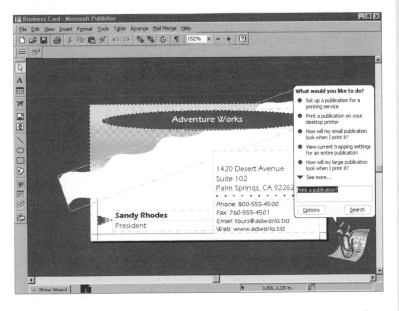

3. Click the *Print a publication on your desktop printer* option to display the Help window shown at the top of the next page.

More about the Office Assistant

If the Office Assistant displays a light bulb above its icon, it has a tip for you. Click the light bulb to see the tip. To move the Office Assistant to another place on the screen, simply drag it. If having the Office Assistant on the screen bothers you or if you would like to customize it, you can click the Office Assistant's Options button to open the Office Assistant dialog box. Here you can select and deselect various options that control such Office Assistant characteristics as when it appears, whether it makes sounds, and what tips it displays. To turn off the Office Assistant permanently, deselect the Use The Office Assistant check box. (Choose Hide The Office Assistant from the Help menu to turn it off temporarily. To make the hidden Office Assistant reappear, choose Show The Office Assistant from the Help menu.) On the Gallery tab, you can click the Back or Next buttons to scroll through the animated characters available for the assistant (the default is Clippit) and then click OK to change the assistant. (You may need to insert the installation CD-ROM to finish the switch.)

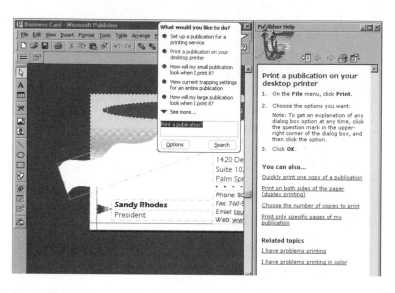

4. Read the information and click *Print only specific pages of my publication* to display instructions for that task.

The Back button

5. Click the Back button to return to the previous window and then explore other options.

To get information without the aid of the Office Assistant, you can display additional help options. Follow these steps:

The Show button

1. Click the Show button to expand the Help window and then click the Index tab to display these options:

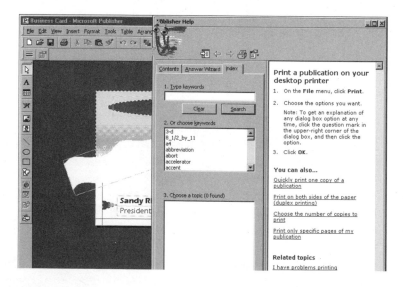

2. In the Type Keywords box, type *prin*. The list below scrolls to display topics beginning with the letters you type.

3. With *print* selected in the Or Choose Keywords list, click Search.

4. Next click *Print a publication on your desktop printer* in the Choose A Topic list to display the help topic that is shown on page 34.

5. Click the Close button to close the Help window.

   We'll leave you to explore other Help topics on your own.

Quitting Publisher

You have seen how to use Publisher to create two simple text-based publications. Easy, wasn't it? All that's left is to show you how to end a Publisher session. Follow these steps:

1. Choose Exit from the File menu.

2. If the Office Assistant asks whether you want to save the changes you have made to the open publication, click Yes.

   Here are some other ways to quit Publisher:

- Click the Close button at the right end of Publisher's title bar.

- Press Alt, then F (the underlined letter in *File* on the menu bar), and then X (the underlined letter in *Exit* on the File menu).

- Double-click the Control menu icon (the *P* with the sheet of paper) at the left end of Publisher's title bar.

Other ways to get help

The Contents tab of the Help window displays various topics represented by book icons and their subtopics represented by question mark icons. To display a topic's subtopics, click the plus sign to the left of the book icon. When you find the subtopic you're looking for, click it. Help displays the information in the right pane. The Answer Wizard provides a way to type search questions without the Office Assistant interface. To access the Answer Wizard, simply display the Help window, click the Answer Wizard tab, type a question in the edit box, and then click Search. Help then displays a list of topics that most closely fit your question. You can then double-click one of the topics to display its contents in the right pane of the Help window. If you have a modem and are connected to the Internet, you can access the Microsoft Publisher Web Site to get information or technical support. Choose Microsoft Publisher Web Site from the Help menu to start your Web browser, connect to the Internet, and display the site's home page.

2

Developing a More Complex Publication

You use a wizard to create a flyer and then rearrange its elements by working with its frames. Then to see how to customize the flyer further, you take a look at Publisher's formatting capabilities, including multiple columns, lists, and styles.

The sample flyer is for a business, but flyers are also a common means of communicating information about organizations, clubs, events, and even family news.

Publication created and concepts covered:

Add a fancy touch with a dropped capital letter

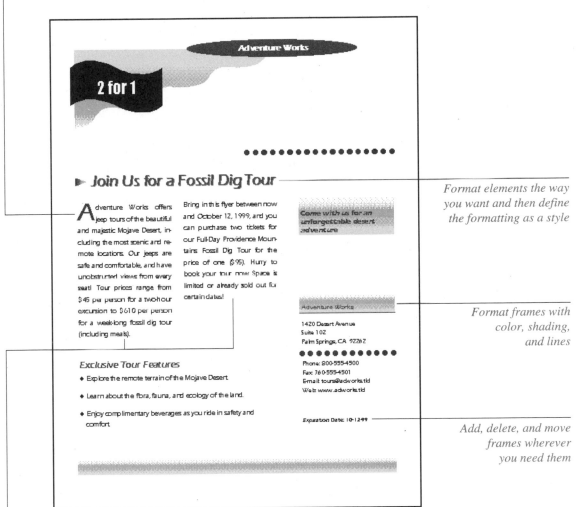

Adventure Works

2 for 1

▶ Join Us for a Fossil Dig Tour

Adventure Works offers jeep tours of the beautiful and majestic Mojave Desert, including the most scenic and remote locations. Our jeeps are safe and comfortable, and have unobstructed views from every seat! Tour prices range from $45 per person for a two-hour excursion to $610 per person for a week-long fossil dig tour (including meals).

Bring in this flyer between now and October 12, 1999, and you can purchase two tickets for our Full-Day Providence Mountains Fossil Dig Tour for the price of one ($95). Hurry to book your tour now. Space is limited or already sold out for certain dates!

Come with us for an unforgettable desert adventure

Adventure Works

1420 Desert Avenue
Suite 102
Palm Springs, CA 92262

Phone: 800-555-4500
Fax: 760-555-4501
E-mail: tours@adworks.tld
Web: www.adworks.tld

Expiration Date: 10-12-99

Exclusive Tour Features

- ◆ Explore the remote terrain of the Mojave Desert.
- ◆ Learn about the flora, fauna, and ecology of the land.
- ◆ Enjoy complimentary beverages as you ride in safety and comfort.

Format elements the way you want and then define the formatting as a style

Format frames with color, shading, and lines

Add, delete, and move frames wherever you need them

Set up a multi-column format to create a "newspaper" look

In Chapter 1, you created two simple publications with very little fuss by using a couple of Publisher's built-in wizards. But as useful as wizards are, they don't always produce exactly the look you want, and you will often want to make adjustments to the frames, add more text, or change the text's formatting. In this chapter, you first use a wizard to create a flyer for Adventure Works. Then you make changes to the publication's frames and adjust the formatting of some of the words and paragraphs to change how the flyer looks. Finally, you define a set of custom text formatting as a style so that you can easily apply the entire set to other parts of your publication.

Using a Design Set to Create a Publication

Most businesses and organizations use a common design and color scheme for all their printed promotional materials so that when people see a promotional piece, they immediately identify it with the business or organization. To make this practice easier, Publisher provides several *design sets*, which organize the wizards used to create publications by design.

Design sets ⟶

Suppose Adventure Works has decided to use the Waves design for all its publications. You have already created an informational postcard and a business card using this design, and now you want to create a flyer to promote a special offer. Follow these steps to access the Flyer Wizard from the Publications By Design tab of the Catalog dialog box:

1. Start Publisher by choosing Programs and then Microsoft Publisher from the Start menu.

2. When the Catalog dialog box appears, click the Publications By Design tab to display the options shown on the facing page. (If you are already working in Publisher, you can display the Catalog dialog box by choosing the New command from the File menu.)

Displaying the Catalog dialog box ⟶

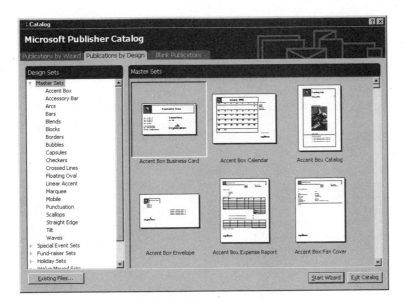

In the Design Sets pane, Publisher lists all its basic designs (the Master Sets), as well as other design sets that have specific themes. (See the tip below for more information.)

The Master Sets

3. Next click Waves in the Master Sets section of the list, and then scroll down the right pane. Notice that Publisher displays all the publication wizards that can use the Waves design template.

4. Double-click Waves Special Offer Flyer to start the Flyer Wizard.

Special design sets

In addition to the design templates in the Master Sets list, you can access several specialized design sets via the Publications By Design tab. (These special design sets can also be accessed via the Publications By Wizard tab.) Special Event Sets and Fund-Raiser Sets each offer three templates geared toward special events or fund-raisers. Holiday Sets includes three templates appropriate for winter holiday occasions. We've Moved Sets has four templates used for change of address announcements or house-warming invitations. Restaurant Sets provides two templates used for menus and other restaurant-related publications. Finally, Special Paper displays nine templates available through a company called PaperDirect, which produces colored and patterned paper. If you use one of these design templates for a publication, Publisher shows you what the publication will look like when printed on the corresponding paper.

5. If Publisher displays a message box telling you it needs to install a graphics filter, click Yes. (You may have to insert the installation CD-ROM; see the tip below.) Your screen now looks like this:

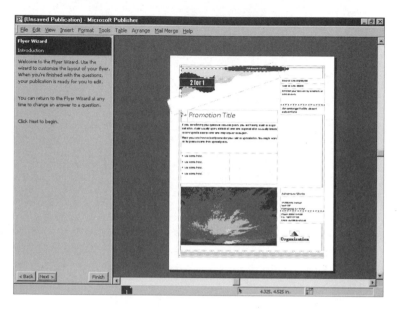

Now let's complete the wizard to create the flyer:

1. Click Next in the wizard's pane to display the list of color schemes, select Tropics, and click Next.

2. Now click No to remove the graphic placeholder and then click Next. (We discuss working with graphics later on in Chapter 3.)

3. Make a note of all the special elements you can add to a flyer. Then check that None is selected in the list, and click Next again to move to the wizard's final dialog box.

4. You don't want to leave a placeholder for a customer address, so with No selected, click Finish.

5. Click the Hide Wizard button to close the wizard and display the new flyer in Publisher's window, as shown at the top of the facing page.

Install on demand

If you try to use a Publisher component or feature that is not installed, Publisher displays a message. To install the missing item, click Yes in the message box. Publisher may prompt you to insert the installation CD-ROM. When the installation is complete, Publisher loads the element or feature. This install on demand capability allows you to install items as you need them rather than having to store items on your hard drive that you may never need to use.

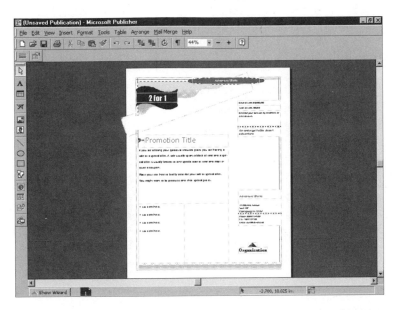

6. Choose Save As from the File menu and save the file as *Flyer* in the My Documents folder.

Before you begin the next section, let's make some adjustments to the personal information set. Follow these steps:

1. Choose Personal Information from the Edit menu to display the dialog box shown earlier on page 9.

Updating a personal information set

2. In the Phone/Fax/E-mail box, click an insertion point at the end of the last line of text, press Enter, and then type *Web: www.adworks.tld*. (While you're at it, you may need to add a hyphen to the word *Email* in the line above.)

3. Double-click the word *An* in the Tag Line Or Motto box, and adjust the entry by typing *Come with us for an*.

4. Finally, change the color scheme for both print and Web publications to Tropics, and click Update.

Reusing Text from Another Publication

Often, you will want to recycle the text from an existing publication in a new one. Suppose you want to use the text from the postcard as the basis for the text in the flyer. Follow the steps on the next page to set up the flyer, and then copy and paste text between the two publications.

1. Change the zoom percentage to 100% (see page 18). If necessary, scroll to the section of the page that displays the Promo-
   tion Title placeholder.

2. Click the placeholder to select its text, and type *Join Us for a
   Fossil Dig Tour*. (Publisher automatically copyfits the text to
   fit in the frame. See the tip on the facing page for more
   information.)

3. Now click the placeholder below the new heading, and with
   all the text in the frame selected, press Delete.

4. Save your changes.

The Open button →

5. Click the Open button on the Standard toolbar to display this
   dialog box:

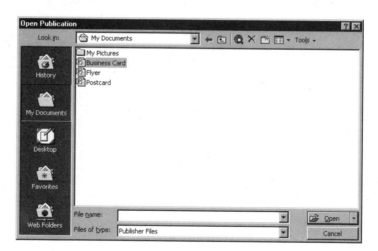

Opening options

In addition to using the Look In box to navigate to the publication you want to open, you can click icons on the
shortcuts bar on the left side of the Open Publication dialog box to display the contents of specific folders in which
you might have saved the publication. You can change the view of the list by clicking the arrow to the right of the
Views button. For example, selecting Preview splits the list pane so that a preview of the file selected on the left is
displayed on the right, allowing you to check visually that you are opening the publication you want. You can also
sort the list of filenames by selecting Arrange Icons from the Views drop-down list. You can click the Tools button
to access commands for finding, deleting, and renaming files; to add a publication to your list of favorites; and to
provide ready access to a computer on a network by mapping its hard drive so that it shows up as a drive letter on
your computer. Finally, you can click the arrow to the right of the Open button to open the selected file as read-
only, meaning you can view it but not change it.

6. Double-click Postcard to open the publication. You can't have more than one file open at a time, so Publisher closes the Flyer publication. (Click Yes if Publisher asks whether to save any changes.)

7. Select all the text that describes the company by clicking an insertion point in its text frame and pressing Ctrl+A. Then click the Copy button on the Standard toolbar.

8. Open the flyer by choosing it from the list of recently opened publications at the bottom of the File menu.

9. Press F9 to zoom to actual size (100%) and click an insertion point in the empty text frame below the heading.

10. Click the Paste button to paste the text from the postcard into the frame.

11. Edit the text so that it looks like the paragraphs shown below. (We've magnified the page so that the text is more readable, and indicated in bold the additions you should type. Obviously, you shouldn't include the bold formatting in your text.)

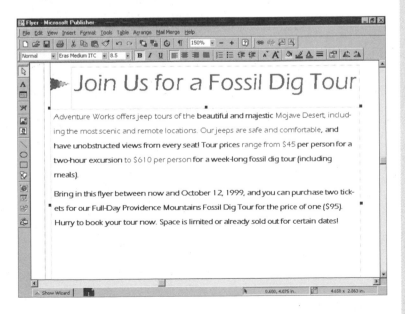

Copyfitting text

If you enter more text than will fit in a frame, the text is stored in a place called the overflow area, and selecting the frame displays the Text In Overflow indicator shown on page 31. You can make the text fit in its frame in several ways. You can manually decrease the text size a little at a time until everything fits, or you can have Publisher perform this task for you by choosing AutoFit Text and then Shrink Text On Overflow from the Format menu. Publisher then reduces the size of the text until there is no longer any text in the overflow area. If you resize the frame and want to make the text fit the new size, you can choose AutoFit Text and then Best Fit. You can also turn on automatic copyfitting to have Publisher make adjustments every time you edit the text, by choosing AutoFit Text and then toggling off None. (To turn off automatic copyfitting, choose AutoFit Text and then toggle on None.)

Working with Frames

You've entered the main text of the flyer, and Publisher has entered information about your company using the Primary Business personal information set. You now want to customize the flyer, but first you need to learn how to work with frames. In this section, you'll see how to size, delete, move, and add frames.

Sizing Frames

In Chapter 1, you decreased the size of the phone/fax/e-mail text so that it would fit in its frame after you added the Web site address. But often you will want to increase the text's size so that it is more legible. When making the text larger means the frame is no longer big enough to display all the text, you can resize the frame. Follow these steps to make the tag line's font larger and then increase the size of its text frame:

1. Turn on the rulers by choosing Rulers from the View menu.

2. Select the tag line (the text that starts *Come with us*) and change the font size to 12. Publisher displays the Text In Overflow indicator shown earlier on page 31.

3. Point to the bottom middle handle of the frame. The pointer displays arrows showing the directions in which you can resize the frame, and the word *RESIZE* appears below the pointer. On the rulers at the top and left sides of the window's

---

More about resizing

You can drag a text frame's corner handles to resize both the height and width of the frame. To resize both dimensions proportionally, hold down the Shift key as you drag. When the frame reaches the size you want, release the mouse button and then the Shift key. (This procedure works only for text frames.)

Special mouse pointers

By default, Publisher displays special mouse pointers when you move the pointer over certain elements of a publication. When you select a frame, the pointer appears as a moving van with the word *MOVE* when it is over the frame's border, and as a set of arrows with the word *RESIZE* when it is over a handle. You might find these pointers a little too cute and want to turn them off, but while you are learning to use Publisher, we recommend that you leave them turned on. Otherwise, it is easy to find yourself moving a frame when you want to resize it, and vice versa. To turn off this feature later, choose Options from the Tools menu, deselect the Use Helpful Mouse Pointers check box on the User Assistance tab, and click OK.

work area, guides attached to the pointer indicate its position on the page.

Pointer guides

4. To enlarge the frame, hold down the left mouse button and drag the bottom middle handle downward until the pointer guide sits at the 4-inch mark on the vertical ruler. The frame now looks like the one below:

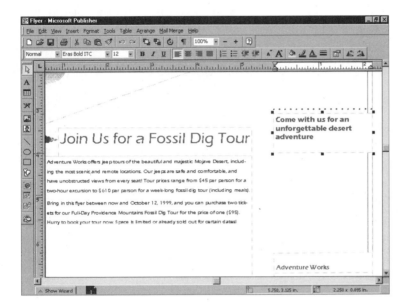

Now change the size of the address and phone/fax/e-mail text by following these steps:

1. Select the address text frame, press Ctrl+A to select all the text, and change the font size to 10.

2. Next select the phone/fax/e-mail text frame, select all its text, and increase its size to 10.

3. Point to the bottom middle handle of the selected frame and drag to the 8½-inch mark on the vertical ruler. The text (including the Web address you added to the personal information set on page 41) now fits in the frame.

4. Save your work.

   From now on, we won't remind you to save, so be sure to click the Save button often to safeguard your work.

Adding and Deleting Frames

Suppose you want to add a subheading before the bulleted list at the bottom of the page. All text must be contained in a frame, so you need to add a new frame to the flyer. You also want to delete a couple of extraneous ones. Follow these steps:

1. Scroll to bring the bulleted-list frame at the bottom of the page into view. (You haven't entered any text here yet, but you will on page 60.)

2. Select the bulleted-list frame, point to the top middle handle, and resize the frame by dragging the handle downward until the top of the frame is at the 8-inch mark on the vertical ruler.

The Text Frame Tool button

3. Click the Text Frame Tool button on the Objects toolbar and move the pointer over the work area. The pointer changes to a cross hair, waiting for you to draw a frame.

4. Point to the blue boundary line on the left side of the page and adjust the pointer's position until the pointer guide on the vertical ruler sits at the 7½-inch mark. Then hold down the left mouse button and drag downward and to the right to draw a new frame about ½ inch tall and the same width as the bulleted-list frame below it. When the frame is the correct size, release the mouse button to insert the frame as shown here:

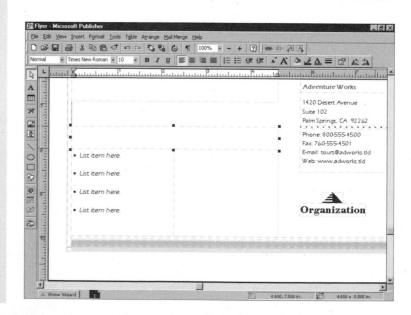

5. Type *Exclusive Tour Features* in the new frame. By default, the font of the text you enter in a new frame is Times New Roman, its size is 10 points, and it is aligned horizontally on the left and vertically at the top of the frame, with no other formatting. (You'll change this formatting on page 51.)

Default formatting

When you use one of Publisher's wizards, the publication you create may contain frames for information you don't want to include. As you saw in Chapter 1, to get rid of these frames, you can simply delete them. Follow these steps:

1. Click the word *Organization* below the phone/fax/e-mail frame to select the Logo placeholder, right-click the selection, and choose Delete Object from the shortcut menu. (We show you how to create a logo on page 70.)

2. Next scroll to the top of the page and delete the time-of-sale frame and the location-description frame.

Moving Frames

Now the flyer includes only the frames you want, but some of the frames would look better in different locations on the page. Follow these steps to move a couple of the frames:

1. With the top of the page still displayed, select all the text in the date-of-sale frame and type *Expiration Date: 10-12-99*.

2. Now point to the frame's top border, but not at one of its handles. The pointer changes to a four-headed arrow with a moving van attached.

3. Hold down the left mouse button and drag toward the bottom of the page. When you reach the bottom of Publisher's window, continue dragging as Publisher scrolls the hidden part of the page upward into view.

4. As long as you hold down the mouse button, guides on the vertical ruler indicate the position of the top and bottom of the frame, and guides on the horizontal ruler indicate the position of the left and right sides. Release the mouse button when the top of the frame sits at the 9-inch mark on the vertical

Ruler options

You can move a ruler by simply dragging it to a new position. To move both rulers at the same time, drag the box where they intersect. To return the rulers to their original positions, simply drag them back. You can move the zero point of a ruler, which normally corresponds to the position of the top left corner of the page displayed on your screen. Point to the location on the ruler where you want the new zero point to be. When the mouse pointer changes to a double-headed arrow, hold down the Shift key and click the right mouse button. To return the zero point to the default position, double-click the ruler. To change the measurement unit, choose Options from the Tools menu, click the arrow to the right of the Measurement Units edit box on the General tab, and select a different option. Publisher then updates the rulers and all dialog boxes that use units of measure.

ruler and the left and right sides of the frame align with the frame above. The result is shown here:

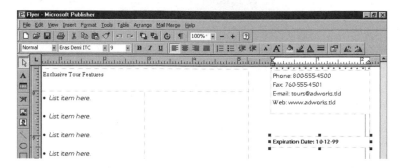

Using the Size And Position Dialog Box

The Flyer Wizard added a frame containing a row of dots between the address text and the phone number text to give the eye a breather between sets of information. However, at their current size, the dots are difficult to see. Let's move the phone/fax/e-mail frame down a bit and then use a more precise method to enlarge and position the frame that contains the dots, so that you can make them bigger. Here are the steps:

Positioning frames precisely →

1. Select the phone/fax/e-mail frame and choose Size And Position from the expanded Format menu to show this dialog box:

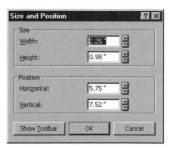

2. In the Position section, click the up arrow at the right end of the Vertical box until it reads *7.72"*. Publisher then adjusts the frame's position on the page, and you can instantly see the results of the new setting. The frame looks good, so click OK.

3. Select the dots frame and choose Size And Position from the Format menu. (If you have trouble selecting the frame, increase the zoom percentage and then click one of the dots.)

4. Enter *0.1"* as the Height setting, and *7.57"* as the Vertical setting. Then click OK. At 100%, this part of the flyer now looks
like this:

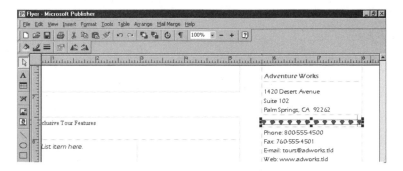

Using Ruler Guides

To help you position and align objects on a page, you can display ruler guides. Follow these steps to fine-tune the position
of the tag-line frame using a ruler guide:

1. Scroll until the tag line comes into view.

2. Hold down the Shift key, point to the horizontal ruler, and
when the pointer changes to a double-headed arrow and the
word *ADJUST* appears, drag downward. When the green line
attached to the pointer aligns with the bottom of the text frame
that contains the flyer's title, release the mouse button and the
Shift key.

3. Using the green line as your guide, move the tag-line frame
downward until the top of the frame aligns with the green line.

4. Check that the right side of the frame still aligns with the
pink layout boundary line and, if it doesn't, adjust the frame
accordingly.

5. To remove the ruler guide, point to it, hold down the Shift
key, and drag upward to the horizontal ruler. When you release the Shift key and the left mouse button, the green line
disappears.

Now adjust the size of the row of dots that are above the tag-
line frame by following the steps on the next page.

Ruler guides vs. layout guides

Ruler guides are displayed in green
and appear only on the page on
which you create them. Layout
guides appear by default on each
page of a publication. The pink
lines are margin guides; four of
them appear at the top, bottom,
left, and right sides of each page
to indicate the publication's margins. The blue lines are grid guides
that divide the page into equal
segments. You use these layout
guides to position frames consis-
tently from page to page and from
publication to publication. To adjust them, choose Layout Guides
from the Arrange menu. You can
then change the position of the
margin guides and display more
or fewer grid guides. To hide all
guides so that you get a better
idea of how a page will look when
printed, choose Hide Boundaries
And Guides from the View menu.
To redisplay them, choose Show
Boundaries And Guides.

1. Select the dots frame and then display the Size And Position dialog box.

2. Enter *3.5"* as the Width setting, *0.1"* as the Height setting, *4.5"* as the Horizontal setting, and *2.94"* as the Vertical setting. Then click OK.

3. Choose Rulers from the View menu to turn off the rulers. Change the zoom setting to 50%, and click a blank part of the work area so that you can see the main features of the flyer, which look like this:

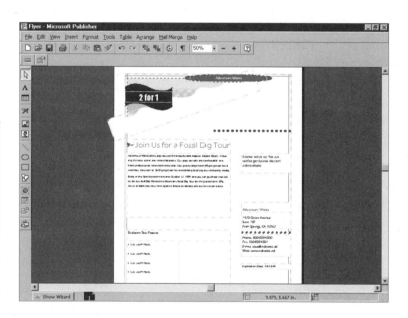

Painting formats

If you apply formatting to a block of text and then want to repeat those settings for another block, you can copy all the formatting in a simple three-step procedure. Select the text with the formatting you want to copy, click the Format Painter button on the Standard toolbar, and then select the text you want to format. Publisher duplicates the formatting for the new selection. To copy the formatting of the text in a frame to another frame on the same page, select the first frame, hold down the right mouse button, and drag to the frame you want to format. When you release the mouse button, choose Apply Formatting Here from the shortcut menu that appears. (If you prefer menu commands, you can use the Pick Up Formatting and Apply Formatting commands on the Format menu.)

Changing the Look of Words and Paragraphs

When you use one of Publisher's wizards to create a publication, the program makes a lot of decisions for you about how various elements will look. However, as you just saw, when you add a new text element to a publication, Publisher applies very little formatting, assuming that you will want to control the appearance of the new element yourself. In this section, we look at a variety of methods for changing the look of words and paragraphs.

Making Headings Stand Out

Headings are the most important elements in promotional publications. Their job is to grab the attention of your readers, draw them in, and make them want to read further. So headings should always be formatted in such a way that they catch the readers' eye. In the previous section, you added a new heading to the flyer. As it is, the heading would likely go unnoticed. Follow these steps to make it stand out:

1. Press F9 to zoom to 100%. Select the Exclusive Tour Features heading, and click the arrow to the right of the Font box on the Formatting toolbar to display a list of the available fonts.

The Font box

2. Scroll the list upward and select Eras Medium ITC to change the font to match the rest of the flyer.

3. Click the arrow to the right of the Font Size box and click 16.

4. Next click the Bold button to make the selected text bold.

The Bold button

5. With the text still selected, right-click it and choose Change Text, Align Text Vertically, and then Bottom from the shortcut menu to align the text vertically along the bottom of the frame. Then click a blank area to see the heading, which now looks like this:

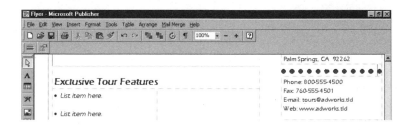

Picas and points

Picas and points are the standard units of measurement used in the publishing world. If you plan to send your publications to outside printing companies, you may need to use picas and points instead of inches when discussing the sizes of certain elements. (A pica is 1/6 inch and there are 12 points in a pica, so a point is 1/72 of an inch.) You might want to use these units of measurement on your rulers and in dialog boxes instead of inches or centimeters. (See the tip on page 47 for more information.) Regardless of what units you use for the rest of your publication, font sizes are always measured in points from the top of ascending letters, such as *h*, to the bottom of descending letters, such as *p*.

Now let's format the other headings in the flyer so that they stand out better as well:

1. If necessary, scroll upward, select *Adventure Works* in the oval, change its size to 14, and then make it bold.

2. Next select the flyer's title and choose Font from the Format menu to display this dialog box:

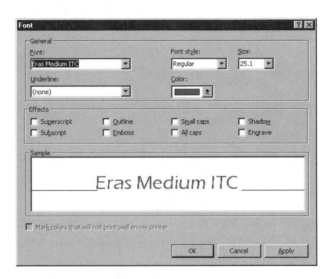

More about fonts

When you print most fonts on paper, they appear the same way they do on the screen because most printer fonts have a corresponding screen font. For those that don't, Publisher chooses the closest match, which can cause layout problems because of differences in character spacing or letter size. Publisher recommends that you use only TrueType fonts, which have both screen and printer components, so that what you see on-screen is what you get on paper. TrueType fonts are identified by a TT symbol to the left of the font name in the font list.

Character spacing

In the publishing world, the adjustment of spacing between characters is called *kerning*. Tighter kerning pulls characters together, and looser kerning pushes them apart. Awkward character spacing is more evident with large text, such as in headlines, so by default, Publisher adjusts the space between certain character pairs when the point size is greater than 14. You can change Publisher's kerning setting or turn it off by choosing Character Spacing from the Format menu. In the Automatic Pair Kerning section, adjust the point size at which kerning kicks in or deselect the Kern Text At check box to turn off automatic kerning altogether. To manually kern a character pair, first select the characters and choose Character Spacing from the Format menu. In the Kerning section, click the arrow to the right of the edit box and select Expand to increase the amount of space between the characters or Condense to decrease the amount of space. Then enter an amount in the By This Amount box. To adjust the spacing of a large block of text, use the Tracking section of the Character Spacing dialog box. To adjust the width of selected characters rather than the spacing between them, use the Scaling section.

As you can see, the settings in the dialog box reflect the character formatting of the selected title. The dialog box also provides several options not available on the Formatting toolbar.

3. Select Bold from the Font Style drop-down list, click Shadow in the Effects section, and then click OK.

If you want, you can experiment with some of the other options in the Font dialog box before moving on.

Adding Borders and Shading

To emphasize a particular frame, you can draw lines above and below or to the left and right of it, or you can surround paragraphs within the frame with borders of various styles. (You can also use BorderArt to surround text frames with graphics; see the tip on page 87.) Put a border around the organization name by following these steps:

1. Select the organization name frame above the address frame (not the one in the oval at the top of the flyer). Click the Line/Border Style button on the Formatting toolbar to display this submenu of options:

The Line/Border Style button

2. Click the thickest of the line-style options to place a thick border around the frame, as shown here:

3. You don't like this effect, so click the Undo button.

Rebreaking headings

As you create headings for your publications, you may find that some of them would be more aesthetically pleasing if they broke to two or more lines or if they broke somewhere other than where Publisher breaks them. To control the breaking of a heading (or any other line of text), click an insertion point at the place where you want the break to occur and press Shift+Enter.

Instead, you'll draw a line across the bottom of the frame to visually separate the company name from the address. Then you'll add some shading to the frame. Follow these steps to add this formatting:

Drawing lines

1. Click the Line/Border Style button again and then click More Styles in the submenu to display this dialog box:

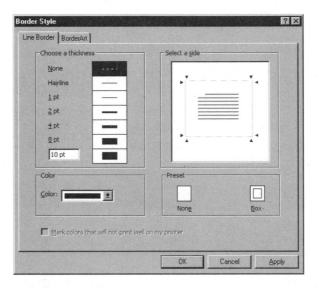

Adding page borders

You can put a border around each page of a publication by clicking the Rectangle Tool button on the Objects toolbar and drawing a rectangle around all the objects on the page. When you release the mouse button, Publisher adds a black, 1-point border. To change the line thickness or color, click the Line/Border Style button and then click More Styles. Select the options you want and click OK. To repeat a border on every page, you can copy and paste the first border to all subsequent pages. To add border graphics rather than lines, you can use BorderArt. (See the tip on page 87 for more information.)

2. In the diagram in the Select A Side section, point to the bottom left corner of the frame and click once. Publisher removes all the arrows except those on either side of the frame's bottom border.

3. Next click the 2 pt line in the Choose A Thickness section. Publisher then adds a line to the bottom of the frame in the diagram.

4. Click the arrow to the right of the Color edit box and click the second box (blue) to make the line's color match the text of the organization name. Then click OK.

Now let's add some shading to the frame. Follow the steps on the facing page.

The Fill Color button

1. With the organization frame still selected, click the Fill Color button on the Formatting toolbar to display this submenu:

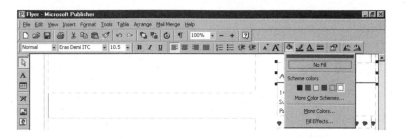

2. Click the third box (gold) in the Scheme Colors section to apply that color to the selected frame.

3. Click the Fill Color button again and then click Fill Effects to display this dialog box:

Adding shading

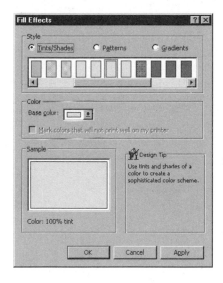

Here you can change the tint or shade of the selected color and apply a pattern or gradient to the shading.

4. Click the Patterns option in the Style section to display the available patterns.

5. If you want, click some of the patterns and note their effects in the diagram below. Then click the solid gold box.

Stick with scheme colors

To change the color scheme, click More Color Schemes on the Font Color button's menu. If you want to use a color that is not part of the current color scheme, you can click the More Colors option to display the Colors dialog box, and then click an area in the color palette and move the slider on the luminescence scale. However, if you use a color from the scheme, your selection will coordinate with the other colors on the slide. If you later decide to change the color scheme, the color you select will then change accordingly.

Adding a pattern or gradient

6. To match the pattern used at the bottom of the flyer, click the Gradients option and select the twelfth gradient pattern. (Click the right arrow on the horizontal scroll bar once and then click the gradient pattern farthest to the right.) Then click OK to implement the changes.

7. Repeat the above steps to apply the same shading color and gradient pattern to the tag-line frame.

Aligning text vertically

8. With the tag-line frame still selected, choose Align Text Vertically and then Bottom from the Format menu so that its text rests along the bottom of the frame. Here are the results at 50%:

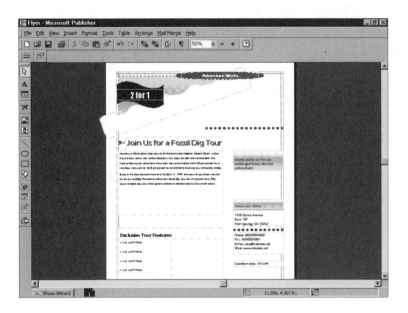

Changing Text Colors

When you add a border or shading, the formatting affects the entire frame. However, when you change the color of text, the change affects only the selected text. Let's change the color of the heading you added earlier:

1. Press F9 and then scroll the *Exclusive Tour Features* heading into view.

The Font Color button

2. Select the heading and click the Font Color button on the Formatting toolbar. Publisher displays a submenu similar to the one shown on the previous page, which you can use to apply

color to the selected text in much the same way you apply it to a frame. You can select one of the current scheme's colors or select a color from a different scheme. You can also select a custom color and add fill effects.

3. If you want, experiment with some of the text effects, and then finish by clicking the second box (blue) in the Scheme Colors section. The color of the heading now matches that of other headings in the flyer.

Adding a Drop Cap

A simple way to add a designer touch to a publication is to use Publisher's built-in *drop cap* (for *dropped capital letter*) format. For example, drop caps are used in the first paragraph of each chapter in this book. You might want to enhance newsletters, reports, and other publications intended for public viewing by adding drop caps. As a demonstration, let's insert a drop cap in the first paragraph of the flyer's main text:

1. Scroll to the paragraph below the flyer's title and click an insertion point to the left of the first line (the one that begins *Adventure Works offers*).

2. Choose Drop Cap from the Format menu to display this dialog box:

Creating custom drop caps

After you select one of Publisher's built-in drop cap styles, you can adjust its formatting on the Custom Drop Cap tab of the Drop Cap dialog box. You can change the number of letters used and the position, size, font, font style, and color of the letter or letters. As you make changes, Publisher displays a sample in the adjacent Preview box. When you click OK, Publisher applies the new drop cap in the specified location and adds the new style to the Drop Cap tab of the Drop Cap dialog box. This way, you do not have to recreate it if you want to use it again.

Publisher displays several drop cap styles in the Available Drop Caps section. You can select any style and view its results in the Preview box on the right. If none of the styles fits your needs, you can create your own drop cap style (see the tip on the previous page).

3. Scroll the Available Drop Caps list to see what's available. Then click the style that is two lines high in the second column, and click OK.

4. To coordinate the drop cap with the rest of the flyer, select the drop cap and then choose Font from the Format menu. Change the font to Eras Medium ITC, the style to bold, and the color to red. Then select Shadow as the Effects option and check that the size is 8.5 before clicking OK. Here are the results:

Setting Up Multiple Columns

Flyers and newsletters often feature multi-column layouts like those used in magazines and newspapers. With these layouts, you have more flexibility in placing elements on the page, and multi-column layouts are often more visually interesting than single-column layouts. To demonstrate how easy it is to set up multiple columns in Publisher, let's change the main text frame of the flyer to a two-column format. Follow these steps:

The Text Frame Properties button

1. Click the flyer's main text frame once to select it. Then click the Text Frame Properties button on the Formatting toolbar to display the dialog box shown on the facing page.

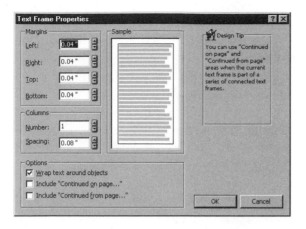

2. In the Columns section, change the Number setting to *2* and the Spacing setting to *0.28"* so that the text will be arranged in two columns with 0.28 inch of space between them. Then click OK.

The flyer would look better if the second paragraph of text started at the top of the second column. You can shorten the frame to force text to flow from the first column to the second, or you can insert a column break. Let's try the break method:

1. First click an insertion point at the beginning of the second paragraph.

Inserting a column break

2. Press Ctrl+Shift+Enter. Publisher inserts a column break and moves the second paragraph to the next column, as shown here:

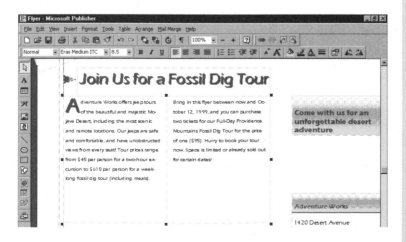

More text frame properties

In addition to changing the number of columns in a particular frame, you can also make other adjustments in the Text Frame Properties dialog box. In the Margins section, you can adjust the amount of space between the frame and its contents. In the Options section, you can select or deselect options that determine whether text in the frame wraps around other objects, and whether a "Continued on page" or "Continued from page" area appears in the frame to help readers move through a multi-frame story.

Inserting a frame break →

To insert a frame break so that the text moves to the next connected text frame instead of to the next column in the same frame, you would press Ctrl+Enter.

Working with Lists

The text frame on the left at the bottom of the flyer contains four bulleted items that are waiting for your text. Publisher has two built-in list formats: one for bulleted lists and one for numbered lists. Here's how to work with a list:

1. Use the scroll bar to move to the bulleted-list text frame and then click the frame once to select it.

2. This frame is set up for two columns, but you want only one. Click the Text Frame Properties button, change the number of columns to *1*, and click OK.

3. If necessary, press Ctrl+A to select the bulleted text. Then type the following, pressing Enter after each line except the last to add a new bulleted item:

    Explore the remote terrain of the Mojave Desert.

    Learn about the flora, fauna, and ecology of the land.

    Enjoy complimentary beverages as you ride in safety and comfort.

Changing the bullet character →

4. Next press Ctrl+A to select all the bulleted items, and then choose Indents And Lists from the Format menu to display this dialog box:

You can choose one of the six suggested shapes or click the New Bullet button to select other options (see the tip below).

5. Select the diamond shape and click OK to change the bullets, as shown here:

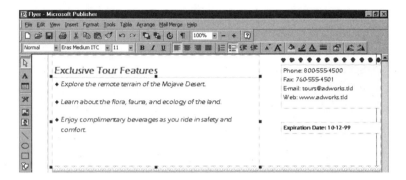

You can quickly convert existing text paragraphs to a bulleted list by selecting the paragraphs and clicking the Bullets button. You can then use the Indents And Lists dialog box to customize the list. If you want to create a numbered list, see the adjacent tip.

The Bullets button

Creating Custom Styles

Every paragraph you write has a *style*. When you create a new text frame in a publication, Publisher automatically applies the Normal style to any paragraphs you enter. As you have seen, the Normal style formats characters with the regular Times New Roman font and makes them 10 points in size. It formats each paragraph as left-aligned and single-spaced. You can change this default appearance of characters and paragraphs by applying different formats one by one, but Publisher provides an easier way. You can define a combination of formatting as a custom style and then apply that combination to a paragraph simply by selecting the style from the Style drop-down list on the Formatting toolbar.

In this section, we'll first show you how to define an existing combination of formatting as a style so that you can apply it to another paragraph in the flyer. Then we'll demonstrate how

More list options

In the Indents And Lists dialog box, you can change the bullet's size, indent, and alignment settings, as well as its character. You can also click the New Bullet button to select a different bullet symbol. (The New Bullet dialog box works like the Insert Symbol dialog box; see the tip on page 73 for information.) To switch to a numbered list, click the Numbered List option in the Indent Settings section. The dialog box changes to display numbered list options, such as the number format and the separator type (a period, for example). To convert the list to regular text, click the Normal option in the Indent Settings section and click OK.

The Style box

to create a style for the main text paragraphs of the flyer from scratch. Follow these steps:

1. Select the *Join Us* title and click the Style box at the left end of the Formatting toolbar once to highlight the name in it.

2. Type *Flyer Title* as the new style name and press Enter to display this dialog box:

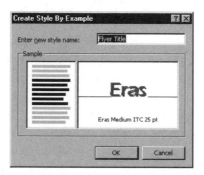

3. Verify that the new style has the correct formatting and then click OK. Publisher creates the style, adds its name to the Style list, and displays Flyer Title in the Style box to identify the style applied to the active paragraph.

Applying a style

4. Click an insertion point in the *Exclusive Tour Features* heading, click the arrow to the right of the Style box to drop down the Style list, and then select the Flyer Title style. Publisher changes the style of the heading so that its formatting is consistent with the title.

5. Suppose you change your mind about applying this style to this heading. Click the Undo button on the toolbar to reinstate the previous formatting.

Now let's turn our attention to the main text paragraphs of the flyer. Suppose you want to change the font, add a little space before each paragraph, and adjust the spacing between lines. Follow these steps:

Creating a style from scratch

1. Click an insertion point in the first main text paragraph of the flyer and choose Text Style from the expanded Format menu to display the dialog box shown on the facing page.

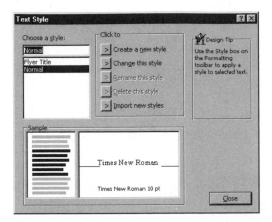

Here you can add a new style; modify, rename, or delete the selected style; or import styles from a different publication.

2. Click the arrow button to the left of the Create A New Style option to display this dialog box:

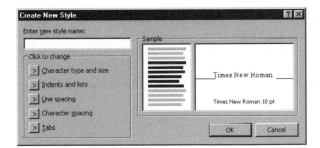

Importing styles

After you create a style for use in one publication, you don't have to re-create it for use in others. Instead, you can simply import the style. Open the publication where you want to use the style, choose Text Style from the Format menu, and in the Text Style dialog box, click the arrow to the left of Import New Styles. In the Import Styles dialog box, navigate to the appropriate publication file and double-click it to import its styles into the current publication. To import styles from a file created in another program, click the arrow to the right of the Files Of Type box in the Import Styles dialog box, select the program the file was created in, navigate to the file, and then double-click it. (If the file type is not listed, you can't import its styles into Publisher.)

Modifying styles

To modify a style, first open the Text Style dialog box and select the style in the Choose A Style list. Click Change This Style to display the Change Style dialog box. Make the necessary formatting changes, click OK, and then click Close to implement the changes. When you redefine a style, all occurrences of that style in your current publication are updated.

3. Type *Flyer Text* in the Enter New Style Name box and then click the arrow to the left of Character Type And Size to display the Font dialog box shown earlier on page 52.

4. Change the font to Eras Medium ITC and the size to 11, and click OK.

5. Next click the arrow to the left of the Line Spacing option to display this dialog box:

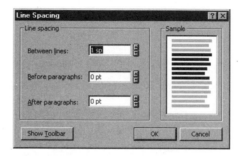

6. Change the Between Lines setting to *1.5 sp* (for *line spaces*) and the Before Paragraphs setting to *3 pt* (for *points*), and then click OK.

7. Click OK again and then click Close to close the other two dialog boxes.

Now let's use the new style to apply some instant formatting:

1. Press Ctrl+A to select all the main text, click the arrow to the right of the Style box, and select Flyer Text. Publisher applies the formatting of the new style to the selected paragraphs but also retains the original formatting of the drop cap you applied on page 57.

2. Because of the new formatting, the text no longer fits in its frame. If necessary, click the tippage that may have appeared, and then drag the frame's bottom middle handle downward about ½ inch until all of the text is visible.

Changing line spacing

You can change the line spacing of any paragraph, not just a paragraph for which you are creating a new style. Click an insertion point anywhere in the paragraph and choose Line Spacing from the Format menu to display the dialog box shown above. Then adjust the Between Lines, Before Paragraphs, or After Paragraphs setting and click OK.

3. With the text of both paragraphs selected, click the Justify
button on the Formatting toolbar as a final touch. Publisher
justifies the paragraphs so that their lines are even with both
the left and right margins. Here are the results at 50%:

The Justify button

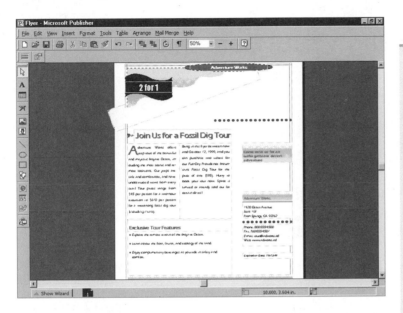

4. To see the results of all your hard work on paper, click the
Print button on the Standard toolbar. The flyer will look like
the one shown on page 37.

You should now have a good grasp of how to work with text
and text frames and of the many ways you can customize
these elements to get the results you want. In the next chapter,
we'll look at how to add graphics and other visual elements to
your publications to give them extra pizazz.

Hyphenating publications

By default, Publisher hyphenates
the text in some text frames, including those you create with the
Text Frame tool. To turn off hyphenation for a particular frame,
select the frame, choose Language
and then Hyphenation from the
Tools menu, deselect the Automatically Hyphenate This Story
check box, and then click OK.
You will want to leave hyphenation turned on if the text is justi-
fied, because it eliminates big gaps
between words. For left-aligned
paragraphs, you can change the
hyphenation zone (the space between the right margin and the
end of the text) by entering a new
measurement in the Hyphenation Zone edit box of the Hyphenation dialog box. If you keep
the hyphenation zone small, the
right side of your text will be less
ragged, but more words will be
hyphenated. If you increase the hyphenation zone, the raggedness
will be more pronounced but
fewer words will be hyphenated.
To manually hyphenate text, deselect the Automatically Hyphenate This Story check box and click
the Manual button. Publisher then
displays each word that can be
hyphenated. Click Yes to hyphenate the word or click No to leave it
unhyphenated.

3
Adding Visual Elements

Publications with interesting graphics grab and hold a reader's attention. This chapter shows you how to add graphics, borders, and special type effects to your publications. You explore Publisher's Design Gallery and use the drawing tools to create your own graphic objects.

In this chapter, you work on a promotional brochure. You can adapt this brochure for any business organization or school group. And you can apply the skills you learn here to make any publication more sophisticated.

Publication created and concepts covered:

Draw a shape, add text, and then manipulate the object in various ways

Work with tables to show numeric information at a glance

Add graphics from the Clip Gallery and size and position them precisely

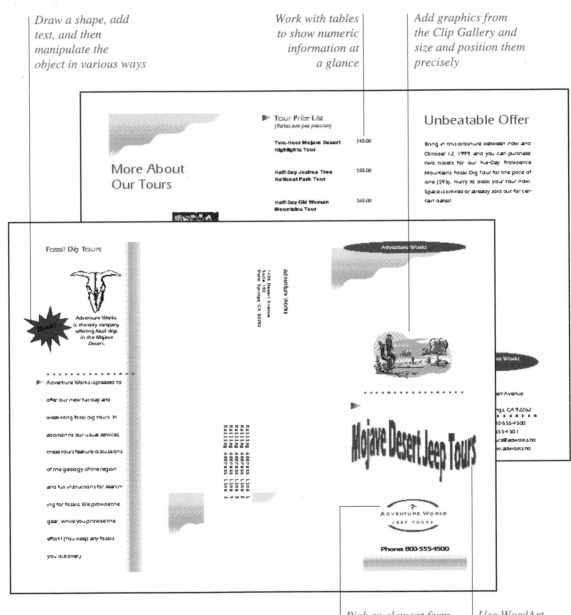

Pick an element from the Design Gallery and then customize it

Use WordArt to create a fancy title

hile following the examples in the preceding chapters, you learned a lot about working with text and text frames and about combining formats to create professional-looking publications. However, words alone are often not enough to get your point across. Most promotional materials include visual elements, either to provide information or to catch the reader's eye.

In this chapter, you create a three-panel brochure for Adventure Works using the Brochure Wizard. We show you how to create special effects with text as you generate a company logo, a fancy title, and a price-list table. Then we demonstrate how easily you can incorporate graphics into your publications. We end the chapter with a discussion of Publisher's drawing tools, which you can use to create your own graphic elements. Let's get started with the brochure:

1. Start Publisher, and when the Catalog dialog box appears, check that the Publications By Wizard tab is displayed.

2. Click Brochures in the left pane and then click Price List to display the designs available for price-list brochures in the right pane.

The Brochure Wizard ⟶

3. Scroll to the Waves Price List Brochure in the right pane and double-click it to start the Brochure Wizard.

4. Click Next to display the color schemes, and with Tropics selected, click Next again.

5. Click Yes to add a placeholder for a customer address, and then click Next.

6. Check that None is selected for the special forms option and click Finish.

7. Click the Hide Wizard button to allocate the entire work area to the brochure.

8. Because you will be working with the brochure's frames, turn on the rulers. The brochure looks as shown at the top of the facing page.

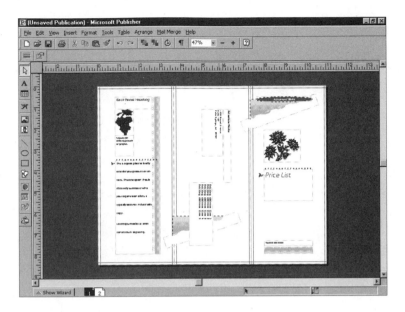

Publisher displays the three outside panels of the brochure. To view the three inside panels, you can click the 2 button in the page controls on the status bar.

9. Save the new publication as *Brochure* in the My Documents folder.

Before you can get started on the visual elements of the brochure, you need to do some quick setup work by adding some text. Follow these steps:

1. Change the zoom setting to 100% and scroll the top of the left panel on the first page into view.

2. Select the Back Panel Heading placeholder at the top of the panel and type *Fossil Dig Tours*.

3. Scroll down, click anywhere in the frame that contains the *This is a good place* placeholder, and type the following text:

   Adventure Works is pleased to offer our new full-day and week-long fossil dig tours. In addition to our usual services, these tours feature discussions of the geology of the region and full instructions for searching for fossils. We provide the gear, while you provide the effort! (You keep any fossils you discover.)

The gibberish in the second paragraph

In the left panel, Publisher has inserted a bunch of nonsense words as the second paragraph. This placeholder text is traditionally used in layout work to give you an idea of how the publication will look when the real text is in place, without distracting you with words you can actually read. We have been unable to discover the origins of this tradition, other than that this block of random Latin words has been used for this purpose for centuries. Interestingly, though the words are Latin, this type of placeholder is known as *greeked text*.

4. Click the 2 button in the page controls and scroll to the top of the left panel.

5. Select the Main Inside Heading placeholder and type *More About Our Tours*.

Rebreaking lines →

6. Click an insertion point to the left of the *O* in *Our* and press Shift+Enter to rebreak the line so that *Our* appears on the second line.

7. Select the text frame below the heading and type the following three paragraphs:

Join us on one of our unique half-day or full-day Mojave Desert jeep tours. You will be accompanied by an expert guide, who will entertain you with fact-filled commentary on the flora, fauna, geology, and history of this fascinating area.

All tours are conducted in air-conditioned, luxury, four-wheel-drive vehicles, each of which is fully stocked with food, beverages, and first-aid kits.

Call today to sign up for the adventure of a lifetime!

8. Save your work.

Adding Visual Text Elements

In the previous chapter, you saw how to format text to make it more visually appealing. But sometimes, this type of text formatting won't be enough. Here, you'll look at a couple of techniques for giving publications more pizzazz. You can then experiment on your own with different ways of combining effects to create the look you want.

Creating a Logo

The Design Gallery →

As you know, Publisher provides many wizards to help you create different types of publications. But the program also has a Design Gallery of elements that you might want to use in more than one publication. In this section, you take a look at the Design Gallery, insert a logo for the cover of the Adventure Works brochure, and then modify it using the Logo Creation Wizard. Let's get started:

1. Move back to page 1 of the brochure and scroll the bottom half of the right panel into view.

2. Click the Design Gallery Object button on the Objects toolbar to display the Design Gallery dialog box, which, as you can see here, is similar to the Catalog dialog box:

The Design Gallery Object button

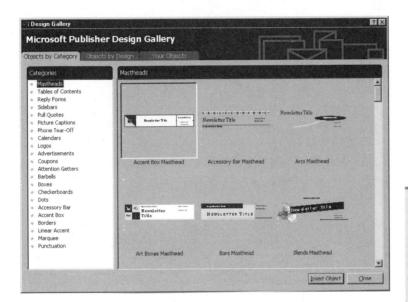

3. In the Categories list in the left pane of the Objects By Category tab, click various headings and check out the options in the right pane.

4. Click Logos in the left pane and double-click Open Oval Logo in the right pane to insert the object on the page, like this:

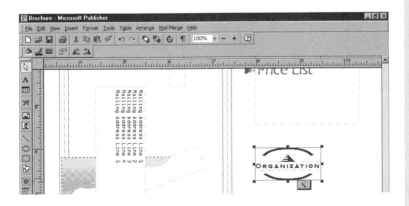

More about the Design Gallery

It is worth taking the time to explore the objects available in the Design Gallery. Included are useful publication elements such as calendars, coupons, and attention getters like the starburst you create from scratch on page 88. On the Objects By Design tab, you can search for items by design template. You can add your own objects to the Design Gallery and then insert them in your publications from the Your Objects tab. To add an object, select it, display the Design Gallery, and click the Your Objects tab. Click the Options button in the bottom left corner and choose Add Selection To Design Gallery from the shortcut menu. In the Add Object dialog box, type a name for the object in the Object Name edit box, select a category from the Category drop-down list or type a name for a new one, and click OK.

5. Click the Wizard button that is attached to the new logo to display a floating Logo Creation Wizard dialog box, like the one shown below:

As you can see, the wizard's dialog box provides options for adding a different logo, changing the logo's design, inserting or removing a graphic placeholder, or changing the number of lines reserved for text.

6. Click Number Of Lines in the top list box, click Two in the pane below, and then click the Close button at the right end of the Logo Creation Wizard title bar.

7. Next select the logo's Organization placeholder and then type *Adventure Works*. (Because of the formatting applied to the placeholder, the words appear in capital letters even though you typed them with only initial capitals.)

8. Increase the zoom setting to 200% and then select the Name placeholder. Type *Jeep Tours* and decrease the zoom percentage again.

9. Next move the logo so that it is centered over the telephone number frame below it, like the one shown at the top of the facing page.

Why doesn't Publisher enter the telephone number?

Publisher enters the telephone number from a personal information set only in phone/fax/e-mail frames. If you point to the frame containing the telephone number at the bottom of the right panel on page 1, you'll see that it is a plain text frame. To insert a phone/fax/e-mail frame, choose Personal Information and then Phone/Fax/E-mail from the Insert menu.

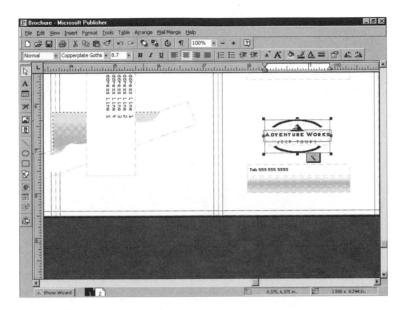

10. Select Tel: and the phone number in the frame below the logo and type *Phone: 800-555-4500*. To make the number more readable, choose AutoFit Text and then Best Fit from the Format menu. Finally, click the Center button on the Formatting toolbar to center the text in its frame.

The Center button

On page 86, we show you how to change the logo's graphic placeholder (the pyramid) and update its color scheme, but for now, let's focus on creating an eye-catching title for the brochure.

Using WordArt for Fancy Type Effects

The cover of the brochure needs a title that grabs your reader's attention, so we'll introduce you to WordArt, a program that ships with Publisher 2000 and Office 2000. You use this handy program to mold text into shapes that fit the mood of a publication or to flow text around other elements on the page. Follow these steps to jazz up the cover of the brochure:

1. Select the Price List frame on the right panel of the first page and choose Delete Object from the Edit menu to delete the frame and its text. (You don't need this frame because you will use a WordArt frame instead.)

Inserting special symbols

To insert a special symbol, such as an accent mark or a pointing hand to draw the reader's attention, position the insertion point and choose Symbol from the Insert menu. Different fonts have different symbols, so you first need to select the desired font. (Wingdings is a good choice if you're looking for cute little pictures.) Then select the symbol and click Insert.

The WordArt Frame Tool button

2. Click the WordArt Frame Tool button located on the Objects toolbar.

3. Use the cross-hair pointer to draw a frame approximately 2 inches high and 2 inches wide below the row of dots. When you release the mouse button, Publisher starts the WordArt program, and your screen looks like this:

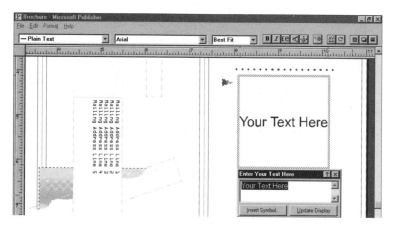

More WordArt options

The WordArt toolbar comes with a variety of buttons, but Screen-Tips doesn't work in WordArt, so you may have trouble deciphering what a particular button will do to your text without actually using the button. Some buttons are toggles, so if you don't like their effects, you can click the button again. Other buttons display dialog boxes in which you give more specific instructions. Some of the effects that can be added to text by clicking the buttons on the WordArt toolbar include equalizing the height of the uppercase and lowercase letters; changing the spacing between characters; rotating, flipping, and stretching the text; and outlining each character.

4. Next replace the text in the Enter Your Text Here box with *Mojave Desert Jeep Tours*. Then click Update Display.

5. Click the arrow to the right of the Shape box at the left end of the WordArt toolbar. (The box currently contains the words *Plain Text*.) Publisher displays this palette of options:

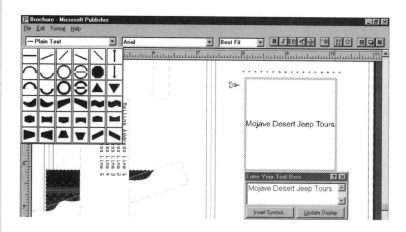

6. Select the fifth shape in the fourth row (Wave 1). Publisher adjusts the text to reflect the wave shape.

7. Change the font to Eras Bold ITC and then click the Shadow button to display this dialog box:

The Shadow button

8. Select the third shadow option from the left and click OK.

9. Next click the Shading button to display this dialog box:

The Shading button

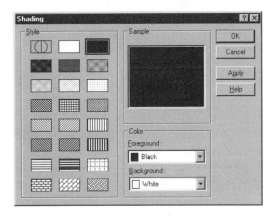

10. Click the arrow to the right of the Foreground box, scroll the list of colors, and then select Red to coordinate the WordArt text color with the publication's color scheme. Click OK.

11. Click anywhere outside the WordArt frame and dialog box to close that program and return to your publication in the Publisher window, which now looks like this:

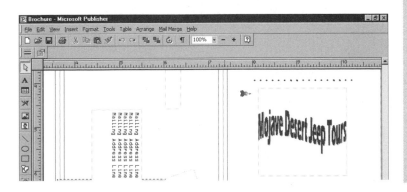

Editing WordArt objects

If you want to make changes to a WordArt object after you have inserted it in a publication, simply double-click the object to open the WordArt program with the text of the object in the WordArt window. You can then edit the text or use the toolbar buttons to make adjustments. When you're finished, click anywhere outside the WordArt frame and dialog box to close the program and update the object in your publication.

Not bad, but the WordArt text looks a little squished. Let's resize the frame:

Sizing WordArt objects

1. Click the title once to select its frame.

2. Use the handles to make the frame shorter and wider, until it looks something like this:

WordArt's capabilities far exceed those demonstrated here. Be sure to read the tips in this section for more ideas, and then try experimenting on your own.

Working with Template Tables

When you first created the Adventure Works brochure, you selected the Price List Brochure design template. The price list brochure includes ready-made tables with placeholders that you can replace to quickly create a price list. Tables are not as exciting as fancy text and graphics, but they are a very important type of visual element. In this section, you'll see how to fill in a template table and how to modify a table to meet a specific need. Follow these steps:

Modifying tables

1. Move to page 2 of the brochure and scroll the top of the middle panel into view.

2. Click an insertion point to the left of the Price List placeholder and add the word *Tour*. Then press End to move to the end of the title, press Enter, and type *(Rates are per person)*.

3. Select the second line of text and change the font size to 9.

4. Click once in a blank area of the first *List your product* frame to select the table, as shown here:

Selecting tables

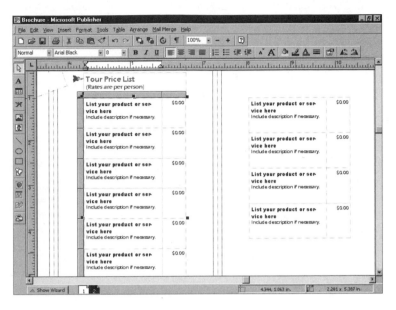

Publisher shows that the table is selected by adding horizontal and vertical gray bars. This particular table has two columns and eight rows, and the insertion point is in the frame at the intersection of the first column and the first row, which is the first *cell* of the table.

5. Select the *List your product or service here* placeholder in the first cell and type *Two-Hour Mojave Desert Highlights Tour*. Notice that as you reach the right edge of the cell, the text automatically wraps to the next line.

6. Select the description placeholder and press Delete.

7. To move to the next cell in the same row, press Tab. Publisher highlights the price placeholder. Type *$45.00* and press Tab to move to the first cell of the second row.

8. Continue filling in the price list by typing the entries shown on the next page, pressing Tab to move from cell to cell. (Pressing Shift+Tab moves the insertion point to the previous cell, and you can also use the Arrow keys and the mouse to move around.)

Moving around tables

Half-Day Joshua Tree National Park Tour   *$55.00*
Half-Day Old Woman Mountains Tour   *$65.00*
Half-Day Turtle Mountains Tour   *$65.00*
Full-Day Providence Mountains Tour   *$95.00*
Week-Long Death Valley National Park Tour   *$495.00*
Week-Long Mojave Desert Fossil Dig Tour   *$610.00*

You don't need the last row in the price-list table. Here's how to delete it:

Deleting rows

1. Point to the vertical gray bar to the left of the last row, and when the pointer changes to a white pointing hand, click once to select the row.

2. Choose Delete Rows from the Table menu.

As a finishing touch for this table, follow these steps to rebreak the lines in some of the cells:

1. In the first cell of the second row, click an insertion point to the left of the word *National* and press Shift+Enter to move the entire word to the second line.

2. Repeat the previous step to move the word *Mountains* to the second line of the first cell in the third, fourth, and fifth rows.

3. Click anywhere outside the table to see the results shown here:

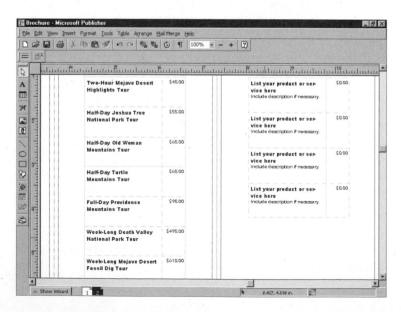

You want only one table in the brochure, so you need to delete the table on the third panel. Follow these steps:

1. With the third panel in view, simply click once anywhere inside the table.

Deleting tables

2. Choose Select and then Table from the Table menu to highlight the entire table.

3. Right-click the selection and choose Delete Object from the shortcut menu.

You want to fill the space formerly occupied by the table with a title and a text paragraph from the flyer you created in Chapter 2. Here's what you do:

1. Copy the title from the first panel by scrolling the panel into view, selecting the *More About Our Tours* frame, and clicking the Copy button on the Standard toolbar.

Recycling text

2. Scroll back to the third panel, and then click the Paste button. Move the title's frame from the middle of the screen so that it top-aligns with the frame of the table's title in the second panel. (You might want to use a ruler guide to help with positioning; see page 49.)

3. Select the title text and type *Unbeatable Offer*. Then resize the frame so that it is as wide and high as the one shown here:

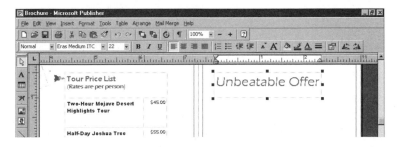

4. Repeat steps 1 and 2 to copy and paste the main text paragraph frame from the first panel to the third pane. Then move the frame below the Unbeatable Offer title and align the two frames.

5. Press Ctrl+A to select all the text in the frame, press Delete, and save your work.

6. Now open Flyer, select the paragraph in the second column of the main text frame, and click the Copy button.

7. Reopen Brochure, paste the paragraph into the new text frame on page 2, and replace the word *flyer* in the first paragraph with the word *brochure*.

8. Press Ctrl+A and change the font size of the new text to 9. Here are the results at 75%:

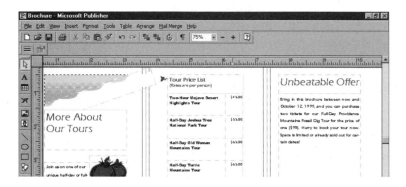

9. Scroll to the address frame at the bottom of the right panel and change the font size to 9. Select all the text in the phone/fax/ e-mail frame, change the font size to 9, and then resize the frame to show all its text, including the Web address.

Adding Graphics to a Publication

Publisher comes with a collection of ready-made graphics files suitable for many different types of publications. You'll use a couple of these "clip art" files in the brochure so you can see how easy it is to import graphics into your publications.

First let's place a graphic on the left panel of page 2 of the brochure. Follow these steps:

1. Scroll to the left panel of page 2 and click the graphic place-holder (the tomatoes) to select it. Publisher selects both the graphic and its caption because they are grouped together.

The All Categories button

2. Double-click the graphic placeholder to display the Clip Gallery window and then click the All Categories button to display the categories shown at the top of the facing page.

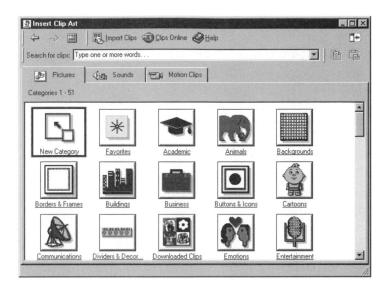

The Clip Gallery stores shortcuts to hundreds of graphics organized in categories on its Pictures tab. (You can also store shortcuts to sound files on the Sounds tab and to video files on the Motion Clips tab.)

Clip Gallery shortcuts

3. Scroll almost to the bottom of the list of categories, and then click the Weather category. The list box changes to display previews of the graphics available in the Weather category, as shown here:

Adding graphics from scratch

Publisher's wizards often insert graphic placeholders in publications. If you want to add a graphic to a page that does not have a placeholder, click the Clip Gallery Tool button on the Objects toolbar and draw a frame on the page where you want the graphic to appear. When you release the mouse button, Publisher displays the Clip Gallery. After you select and insert a graphic in the frame you've drawn, you can move, resize, or customize it as usual.

4. Scroll the previews to check out what's available. (You can click the Keep Looking button at the bottom of the list to display more options, and then use the Back button on the window's toolbar to redisplay the first 60 clips.)

5. Point to any graphic. A pop-up box displays the keywords that describe the graphic, its size, and its graphic format.

The Insert Clip button

6. As a demonstration, click the third graphic in the first row to display a menu of buttons. Click the Insert Clip button to add the graphic to the brochure, and click the Clip Gallery's Close button. The brochure now looks like this:

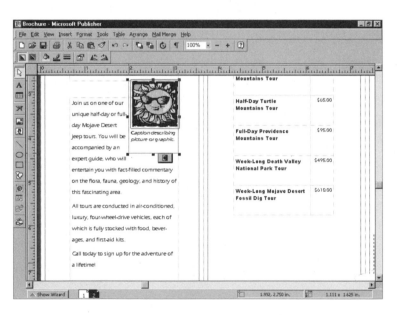

7. To give the graphic a caption, select the caption placeholder and type *Enjoy clear skies and sunshine almost year-round.*

Searching for Graphics

This graphic looks pretty good, so let's track down other suitable images. When you first opened the Clip Gallery, you might have noticed the Search For Clips box. Clip Gallery stores its graphics with a few descriptive terms, called *keywords*, attached. (To see a list of all the keywords attached to a graphic, you can right-click it, choose Clip Properties from the shortcut menu, and check the list on the Keywords tab.) Rather than scroll through the hundreds of graphics in

Other graphic options

The other buttons that become available whenever you select a graphic in the Clip Gallery allow you to preview the selected graphic in a separate window, add a shortcut to the clip to the Favorites category or any other Clip Gallery category, and find similar clips. (See the tip on page 84 for more information.)

the Gallery, you can enter a word or two in the Search For Clips box to locate a specific clip art graphic. Let's look for a graphic that symbolizes fossils and insert it on the left panel of the brochure's first page. Follow these steps:

1. Move to the left panel of page 1, scroll the graphic place-holder (the grapes) into view, and double-click it to display the Clip Gallery.

2. Click the Search For Clips edit box to highlight its contents, type *bones*, and press Enter to display the results shown here:

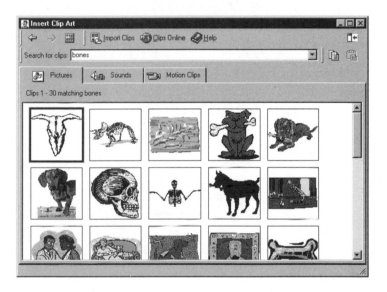

Searching for clips online

If you are hooked up to the Internet, you can click the Clips Online button on the Clip Gallery window's toolbar to access additional clips available on a page of Microsoft's Web site. After you click Clips Online, Publisher starts your Web browser and connects you to Microsoft's Clip Gallery Live Web site. (You may be prompted to connect to the Internet.) Read through the Terms Of Agreement message and then click the Accept button to display the Clip Gallery Live page. Follow the instructions on the page to search for and download a graphic that suits your needs. The downloaded graphic is then automatically added to the Downloaded Clips category and any other applicable categories of the Clip Gallery.

Importing graphics

To insert a graphics file from a source other than the Clip Gallery, click the Picture Frame Tool button on the Objects toolbar and draw a frame where you want the picture. Double-click the new frame, go to the graphics file you want to insert, and double-click it. Publisher can import a variety of graphics formats; check the Files Of Type drop-down list in the Insert Picture dialog box to see them.

If the results of a search don't identify a graphic you can use, you can enter a different word in the Search For Clips edit box.

3. Click the first graphic in the first row, click the Insert Clip button, and then close the Clip Gallery.

4. Repeat the previous steps to search for and insert a graphic on the right panel of the first page using the word *desert*. (We chose the desert scene in the second row.)

Sizing and Positioning Graphics

Like other objects in Publisher, you can easily resize and relocate clip art graphics in a publication. Follow these steps to reposition the desert graphic and change the size and location of the bone graphic:

1. With the desert graphic selected, point to it and drag to the right until the graphic is centered over the row of dots.

2. If necessary, change the zoom setting to 100%, and then select the bone graphic by clicking it.

3. To increase the graphic's height and width, point to the top right handle. When the pointer changes to a double-headed

Finding similar clips

If you see a graphic with a style you like in the Clip Gallery, you can click the graphic and then click the Find Similar Clips button. The button menu expands to let you specify if you want to find graphics with a similar artistic style, similar color and shape, or similar content as defined by the keywords assigned to each graphic. (You can collapse the menu again by clicking the two arrows in the top left or top right corner.) After you make your selection, the Clip Gallery window changes to display graphics that meet your specification.

Adding scanned images

As with a graphics file, you can easily import a scanned image into a publication. (Scanning creates a digital representation of the image that is stored as a graphics file.) First draw a picture frame (see the tip on the previous page). Then double-click the frame to display the Insert Picture dialog box, select the file containing the scanned image, and click Insert. You can then move, resize, and crop the image like any other imported graphic. If a scanner is attached to your computer, you can insert a scanned image into a publication directly from the scanner. Insert the image you want to scan in the scanner, select the graphic frame in the publication, and choose Picture and then From Scanner Or Camera from the Insert menu. Then choose Acquire Image. Use your scanner to scan the image and make any adjustments you want. When you finish, quit the scanning program, and the scanned image will appear in the publication. If you don't have a scanner, you can take photographs or other images to a copy center or photo lab to have them scanned, and then import them as outlined above.

arrow, drag up and to the right to increase both the height and width about ½ inch.

4. Next point to the graphic and drag it to the right until the right edge of the graphic and caption frames sit at about the same point on the horizontal ruler as the right edge of the text frames above and below.

To fine-tune the placement of the graphic and its caption, you can use the Size And Position dialog box as described earlier on page 48. You can also nudge the frames. Let's try the second method:

1. Choose Nudge from the expanded Arrange menu to display the dialog box shown here:

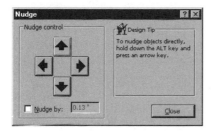

Nudging into position

Scaling graphics

To make a graphic smaller or larger, you resize the graphic's frame, and Publisher scales the graphic to fit the new frame size. You can also scale a graphic to a specific percentage, and Publisher resizes the frame accordingly. To scale a graphic, select it, choose Scale Picture from the Format menu, enter a percentage in the Scale Height or Scale Width edit boxes, and click OK. (If you click the Original Size check box, Publisher enters 100% in both edit boxes.)

Cropping graphics

To display only a specific part of a graphic, you make the graphic's frame smaller without scaling the graphic, so that the part of the graphic you don't want to see is hidden, or *cropped*. For example, to crop ½ inch off the right side of the desert graphic, select the graphic and then click the Crop Picture button on the Formatting toolbar to change the pointer to a cropping tool. Position the cropping tool over the middle handle of the right side and drag to the left ½ inch. To deactivate the cropping tool pointer, simply click the Crop Picture button again.

Controlling text flow

By default, text flows around a graphic frame. To have text flow around the actual graphic, click the Wrap Text To Picture button on the Formatting toolbar. Click the Edit Irregular Wrap button and use the handles around the graphic to adjust how lines of text break. To return to the defaults, click the Wrap Text To Frame button. To adjust how close text gets to the frame, click the Picture Frame Properties button. With Entire Frame selected, adjust any margin; or with the Picture Only option selected, adjust the margin for the entire graphic.

2. If necessary, move the dialog box by dragging its title bar until you can see the graphic.

3. Next use the appropriate arrow buttons to nudge the graphic and caption frames so that their right edges are exactly aligned with the right edge of the other text frames on the panel. Then click the Close button.

4. Select the Caption placeholder and type *Adventure Works is the only company offering fossil digs in the Mojave Desert.*

5. Center the caption and rebreak the first line to the left of *is* and the fourth line to the left of *Desert*.

6. Next click outside the graphic to deselect it. Here are the results at 75%:

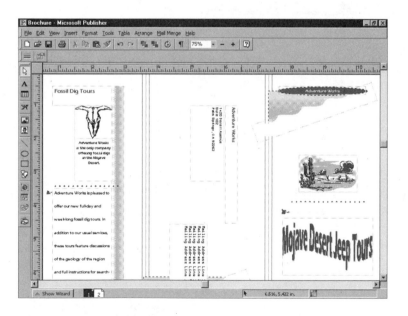

Changing Graphic Colors

As you'll recall, you added a logo to the front panel of the brochure on page 70. However, you still need to replace the logo's graphic placeholder and change the graphic's color. Follow the steps on the facing page.

1. Zoom to 200% and scroll the logo into view. Then double-click the graphic placeholder (the pyramid) to display the Clip Gallery, click the All Categories button, and then click the Navigation Controls category. ← Changing the logo graphic

2. Click the stylized black-and-white compass symbol in the first row, click the Insert Clip button, and then close the Clip Gallery.

3. With the graphic still selected, right-click it and choose Change Picture and then Recolor Picture from the shortcut menu. You see this dialog box:

4. Click the arrow to the right of the Color edit box and select the blue box. Publisher changes the graphic's colors in the Preview box so that you can see the effects of your change.

5. Try the other colors, finishing up with red. Then click OK.

Now let's recolor the rest of the logo using the blue of the Tropics color scheme. Follow the steps on the next page.

BorderArt

Another way to add a visual element to your publications is to use Border-Art, which puts graphic borders around selected objects. Select the frame you want to put the border around, click the Line/Border Style button on the Formatting toolbar, and click More Styles. In the More Styles dialog box, click the BorderArt tab. Select a border graphic from the Available Borders list, and then adjust the border size and colors as necessary, noticing the effects in the Preview box on the right. If none of the styles fit your needs, click the Create Custom button to select a graphic from the Clip Gallery or another source. (Only simple graphics are candidates for BorderArt.) Give the new custom border a name and then click OK to add it to the Available Borders list. You can also delete or rename any border in the list by selecting it and clicking the appropriate button.

Borders around graphics

Some Clip Gallery graphics come with borders around them and some don't. To surround a graphic (or any other object) with a border, click the Line/Border Style button and then make a selection from the available styles. You can also click More Styles to display the Border Style dialog box, select a line thickness, select a color, and click OK.

Recoloring shapes

1. Click the bottom curved line once to select it. (It will be surrounded by a pink frame.)

2. Click the Fill Color button on the Formatting toolbar and then select the blue box. Publisher changes the inside color of the shape but leaves the border black.

3. To change the border, click the Line/Border Style button on the Formatting toolbar, and then click More Styles. Finally, select blue from the Color drop-down list, and click OK.

4. Repeat steps 1 through 3 to change the top curved line's colors.

5. To change the text color, select *Adventure Works*, click the Font Color button on the Formatting toolbar, and select blue.

6. Repeat step 5 to recolor *Jeep Tours*. Here are the results:

Additional shapes

If you hold down the Shift key when you are using the Line Tool, Oval Tool, or Rectangle Tool button, you can draw straight horizontal or vertical lines, circles, or squares. To create arrows, first draw a line with the Line Tool button and then add an arrowhead by using the appropriate arrow button on the Formatting toolbar. (You can add a left arrowhead, a right arrowhead, or both.) To fine-tune the arrow, click the Line/Border Style button and then click More Styles to adjust the thickness, color, and arrow type. To remove an arrowhead, select the line and then click the appropriate arrow button on the Formatting toolbar to toggle it off.

Using the Drawing Tools to Create Graphic Shapes

So far you have used only a few of the buttons on the Objects toolbar. In this section, we'll discuss some of the tools for drawing shapes. For this example, you'll add a starburst shape to draw attention to the new Adventure Works fossil dig tours. (You can draw several other shapes, including ovals, rectangles, and arrows; see the adjacent tip for more information. Also check the Design Gallery before creating your own shapes, because the one you need may already be available!) Let's get going:

1. Press F9 to zoom to actual size and scroll the bone graphic on the left panel into view.

2. Click the Custom Shapes button on the Objects toolbar to display a palette of shape options.

3. Click the fourth shape in the fifth column and then position the cross-hair pointer so that the pointer guides sit at the ½-inch mark on the horizontal ruler and the 1½-inch mark on the vertical ruler.

4. Finally, drag down and to the right until the shape is about 1 inch by 1 inch.

Grouping Objects

All the elements of a publication—text frames, graphics, shapes, color blocks, and so on—are collectively known as *objects*. When you want to be able to move, resize, or rotate two or more objects simultaneously, you group them together. In this case, you want to add a text frame in the middle of the starburst and then group the shape and the text frame. Follow these steps:

1. Click the Text Frame Tool button on the Objects toolbar and drag the cross-hair pointer to create a text frame in the middle of the starburst.

2. With the insertion point in the new frame, type *New!*, format the text as Eras Bold ITC, and size it to fit within the frame.

3. Now select the starburst frame by clicking one of the graphic's lines, and add the text frame to the selection by holding down the Shift key and clicking inside the frame. The objects look like this:

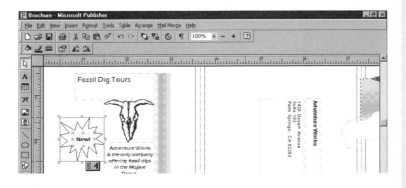

Microsoft Draw

If none of the shapes you can create from the Objects toolbar fit the bill, you can draw your own shapes using Microsoft Draw. To create a drawing for the current publication, choose Picture and then New Drawing from the Insert menu. Then Draw starts from within Publisher and displays a blank frame. Use the Line, Arrow, Rectangle, and Oval buttons on the Drawing toolbar to draw those shapes, and use the buttons on the AutoShapes toolbar to create more complex shapes. The remaining buttons on the Drawing toolbar allow you to manipulate your drawing in a variety of ways. For example, you can change its color and orientation on the page. To return to the publication, click outside the Draw frame. You can then manipulate the drawing's frame just like any other frame. To make changes to the drawing, simply double-click its frame to restart Draw.

The Group Objects button

4. Click the Group Objects button attached to the selection to group the two frames. The objects are now surrounded by one frame, and it is no longer possible to move or resize the graphic without moving or resizing the text, and vice versa.

5. The shape is a little too close to the bone graphic, so drag it down and to the left a bit.

Ungrouping objects

The Group Objects button has become the Ungroup Objects button. You can click this button if you decide the two objects no longer need to be grouped, or if you want to manipulate one object but not the other.

Rotating Objects

What if you want to rotate an object so that it sits at a slight angle? Easy! Try this:

The Custom Rotate button

1. With the grouped object selected, click the Custom Rotate button on the Standard toolbar to display this dialog box:

You can click one of the directional arrow buttons to rotate the object, or you can enter a precise rotational angle in the Angle edit box. To straighten up a rotated object, you can click the No Rotation button.

Flipping objects

In addition to rotating objects, you can flip them all the way over horizontally or vertically. Simply select the object and click the Flip Horizontal or Flip Vertical button on the Formatting toolbar. To quickly rotate an object 90 degrees to the right or left, you can click the Rotate Right or Rotate Left buttons on the Formatting toolbar.

2. If necessary, move the dialog box so you can see the object. Then click the left directional arrow button three times and click Close.

3. How about rotating the object a little further? Instead of using the Custom Rotate dialog box, hold down the Alt key, point to one of the object's handles, and drag counterclockwise to

rotate the object to the left. When you deselect the object, it looks like this:

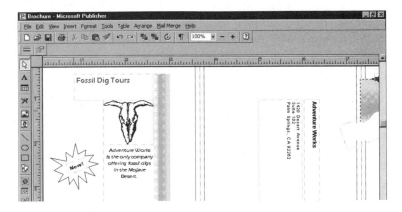

Not bad. But let's give the object some color:

1. Select the object, click the Fill Color button on the Formatting toolbar and select red. Depending on where you clicked to select the object, Publisher fills in either the text frame or the starburst, but not both. (Formatting changes are still made on a frame by frame basis, even though the objects are grouped together.)

Coloring objects

2. Select the other component of the grouped object and change its fill color to red.

3. Click outside the object to deselect it, and then choose Hide Boundaries And Guides from the View menu. The starburst looks something like this:

Hiding on-screen guides

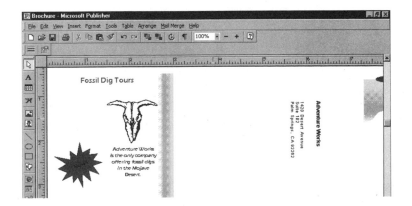

Displaying on-screen guides ⟶
4. Choose Show Boundaries And Guides from the View menu to redisplay these guides for your next project.

5. If you want, click the Print button to see the results of all your hard work on paper.

6. To get a better overview of the brochure's layout, place the two printed pages back to back and fold the brochure into three panels.

7. Finally, save and close the Brochure file.

With WordArt and all the clip art Publisher supplies, as well as graphics from other applications and Publisher's many drawing tools, you shouldn't have trouble adding a dash of excitement to all your publications. Just remember to keep things simple; otherwise, your audience might start paying more attention to your artwork than to the content of your publication.

TWO

BUILDING PROFICIENCY

In Part Two, you build on the skills you gained in the first half of the book. In Chapter 4, you learn design and editorial concepts as you create a newsletter. In Chapter 5, you develop a press release template with foreground and background layers and a custom color scheme. In Chapter 6, you take care of final details, including the proofing and page adjustments that will make your publications both attractive and accessible. You then use Publisher to create a simple Web page that can be used to make information available over the Internet.

Designing a Longer Publication

While showing you how to create a newsletter, we discuss the design and editorial concepts you need to know to produce effective longer publications. Then you learn how to develop and format tables from scratch, and how to work with forms.

The design and editorial techniques you learn in this chapter can be applied to any type of newsletter, such as one you might produce for your school, community group, or business.

Publication created and concepts covered:

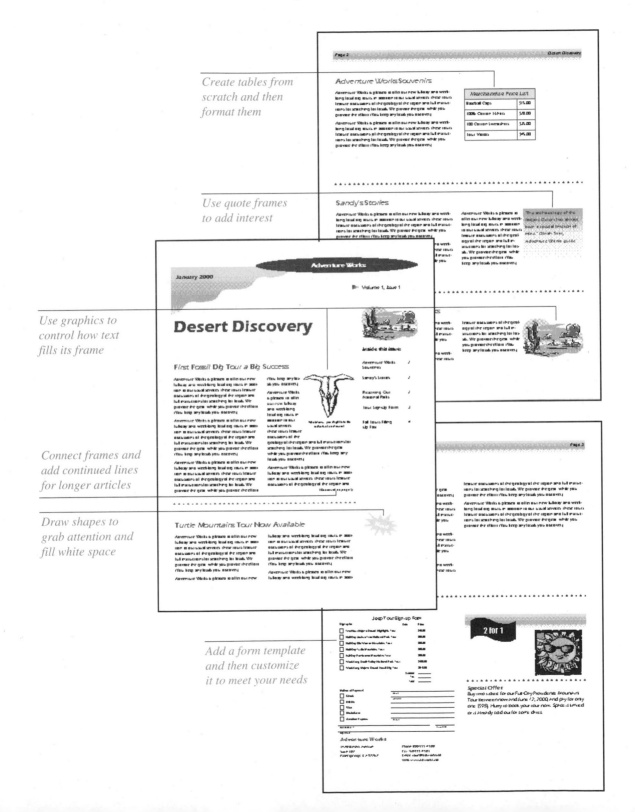

Create tables from scratch and then format them

Use quote frames to add interest

Use graphics to control how text fills its frame

Connect frames and add continued lines for longer articles

Draw shapes to grab attention and fill white space

Add a form template and then customize it to meet your needs

In Part One, you worked with several types of short publications, giving you a good foundation to begin working with Publisher. Because you created publications using Publisher's wizards, you had to do very little design work. However, when you create longer publications, design and editorial issues become much more important. For example, if a publication includes several articles, you must decide in what order to place them and how the text of each article should flow on each page. Depending on the type of publication, you might also need to incorporate graphics, tables, or forms into the publication.

Many businesses and organizations use newsletters to relay information or to advertise new products or ideas. In this chapter, we show you how to create a monthly newsletter for Adventure Works. You start by using a wizard to set up the newsletter, and then we discuss the design decisions you need to make when creating a multi-page publication. As you add text, we discuss the editorial decisions you need to make when fitting text in frames, flowing text from one frame to another, and filling blank areas with graphics and other artwork. Finally, you add a table and sign-up form to the newsletter. As you'll see, even if you don't anticipate ever publishing a newsletter, you can apply the concepts discussed in this chapter to any long publication.

First you need to use the Newsletter Wizard to create the newsletter. Follow these steps:

The Newsletter Wizard

1. If necessary, start Publisher. Click Newsletter and then double-click Waves Newsletter on the Publications By Wizard tab of the Catalog dialog box to start the Newsletter Wizard.

2. Answer the wizard's questions and respond to any messages, selecting the Tropics color scheme, a 2-column format, a customer address placeholder, and a double-sided layout for the publication. Then click Finish.

3. When you finish making your selections, keep the Newsletter Wizard window open and click the 2 button in the page controls to display the second and third pages of the newsletter in the publication window.

4. Click Inside Page Content in the top pane of the Newsletter Wizard window to display its options in the bottom pane.

5. Click the arrow to the right of the edit box in the bottom pane and select Right Inside Page from the drop-down list. Then click the Sign-Up Form With 1 Story option to change the layout of the right page.

Adding a form

6. Click the Hide Wizard button. The two inside pages of the newsletter look like this:

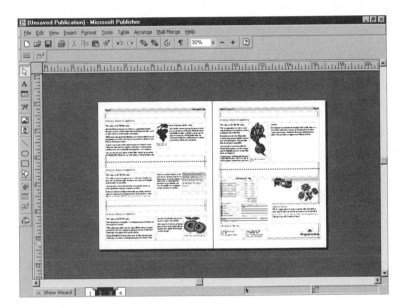

In the publishing world, two facing pages are called a *spread*. When you design longer publications, you will want to look at spreads to see how the pages balance. (You'll learn more about this on page 107.)

Spreads

7. Save the file as *Newsletter* in the My Documents folder. (Remember to save frequently from now on.)

8. Move to page 1 and change the zoom setting to 100%.

Design Decisions

Before you begin making design decisions about the newsletter, you must first work out the details of its contents. Even though you can change elements later if they aren't working for you, it's best to have the most important issues ironed out beforehand. Here are some basic guidelines to follow when developing a longer publication:

- **The audience.** Determine the type of audience you are trying to attract so that you can make decisions about the tone, language level, and graphics you will use.

- **The content.** Decide what information you want to include, and which elements are most important.

- **The visual enhancements.** If you have several graphics available, determine which ones best enhance your stories.

Once you have carefully thought things through, you can begin laying out the publication.

Determining the Type of Audience

Before you spend time, and perhaps money, to get your message out to the world, it makes sense to know as much as possible about your target audience. Here are a few questions to ask about your readers:

- **Their age.** How old are they? The answer to this question influences the reading level and language of your stories, but it is also a major consideration when you are determining how the newsletter should look.

- **Their needs.** Does what you have to offer meet a need or satisfy a desire? The answer to this question determines whether your design and tone are straightforward and down-to-earth, or exciting and evocative.

- **Their characteristics.** Do your readers have common interests, opinions, hopes, or fears? The answer to this question influences the topics you discuss and how you discuss them. If you don't know the answer and you want to appeal to the broadest possible audience, you'll want to keep your discussions general and steer clear of controversial topics.

- **Their level of interest.** Have your readers already indicated an interest in what you have to say? The answer to this question determines how persuasive the newsletter must be and

Printing options

When making design decisions about your publications, you also need to consider your printing options, including type of paper, color or black ink, print quality, and so forth. If you are using a printing service, discuss these issues with your printer before you start work on a publication. (We discuss using a printing service in more detail in Chapter 6.)

how quickly you must convince your readers that they should spend time reading it beyond the first headline.

- **Their level of knowledge.** What do your readers already know about this topic in general and about your organization, service, or product in particular? The answer to this question has some bearing on the amount of space you will dedicate to background information and whether you can use jargon.

By answering these and any other questions you can think of about your audience, you can focus your efforts so that your publications achieve the maximum results. For example, suppose the Adventure Works newsletter will be sent to all past customers, whose ages vary widely, who have taken at least one jeep tour for fun, who have demonstrated an interest in the desert, and who know about the company and its products. This newsletter would likely be quite different from one aimed at attracting senior citizens who have never taken a jeep tour before, who are concerned about their safety and comfort, who think deserts are sandy expanses devoid of plant and animal life, and who have never heard of Adventure Works.

Determining What's Most Important

Armed with information about your audience, you can move on to decide which of the items slated for inclusion in the newsletter are most important and should appear most prominently. Suppose Adventure Works wants the newsletter to drum up repeat business, but also hopes it will generate some referrals. For the premiere issue, you have decided to emphasize the new fossil dig tours by including an article about them on the front page to appeal to existing customers. You will also include information about the company's other tours in case existing customers pass on the newsletter to potential new customers. Start by adding the information for the newsletter's masthead and a heading for the lead article:

1. Scroll to the top of the newsletter, click the Newsletter Date placeholder, and type *January 2000*.

2. Select *Adventure Works* in the oval and change the font size to 14 and the style to bold so that the company name clearly stands out on the front page.

3. Click the Newsletter Title placeholder and then type *Desert Discovery*. Then change the title text to Eras Bold ITC and the size to 36.

4. Click the Lead Story Headline placeholder and type *First Fossil Dig Tour a Big Success*. Here are the results:

All the key elements on the first page now stand out well, and you've designated the fossil dig tours story as the lead article, which lets past customers know what's new and exciting at Adventure Works. Let's allocate space for the other articles:

Two-page view

By default, Publisher displays a multi-page publication in two-page view. When you click the 2 button to move from page 1 to page 2 of the newsletter, Publisher displays pages 2 and 3, the next two-page spread. To display one page at a time, choose Two-Page Spread from the View menu to toggle off the command. But remember to closely scrutinize your two-page spreads for balance before sending them off to the printer.

1. Scroll down the page, select the Secondary Story Headline placeholder, and type *Turtle Mountains Tour Now Available*. You don't expect this tour to be as popular as the fossil dig tours, but leave the text size and spacing of the heading the same as the lead story's for consistency. The story's lower position automatically makes it less important.

2. Click the 2 button to move to the inside spread, and then scroll up and to the left to display the top of page 2.

3. Adventure Works sells shirts and hats, and you want to advertise them in an article at the top of this page. Select the Inside Story Headline placeholder and then type *Adventure Works Souvenirs*.

4. Next replace the second Inside Story Headline placeholder with *Sandy's Stories* and the third headline placeholder with *Preserving Our National Parks*.

5. Scroll to page 3 and replace the top Headline placeholder with *Fossil Dig Tours*. (The story that starts on page 1 will continue here.)

6. Click the 4 button to move to page 4, scroll toward the bottom of the page, and replace the Back Page Story Headline place-holder with *Fall Tours Filling Up Fast*.

Determining Which Graphics to Use

That takes care of all the story headlines. Now you need to decide which stories will have accompanying graphics or graphic elements so that you have a good idea of the potential layout before you add the text. Follow these steps:

1. Click the 1 button to move to the first page. Then zoom to 75% and scroll to get an overview of the page's layout.

2. You want to keep all the elements on this page except the Special Points Of Interest frame. Right-click the frame and choose Delete Object from the shortcut menu.

3. Move to page 2 and delete the grouped graphic/caption accom-panying the Adventure Works Souvenirs story to allow space for a table that lists the available souvenirs and their prices. (You'll create this table on page 112.)

4. Notice the shaded frame to the right of Sandy's Stories. This frame contains a quote placeholder, which will help draw the reader's eye to the story, so leave the frame in place.

5. On page 3, delete the grouped graphic/caption that accompa-nies the continuation of the Fossil Dig Tours story. (You have only one graphic for this story, and it appears on page 1.)

6. Now switch your attention to the logo in the bottom right corner of page 3. Several graphic elements appear in this area of the page, and the logo is featured on the back page of the newslet-ter. You don't need the logo here, so select it and delete it.

Using visual elements to end stories

Newsletters and magazines often designate the end of articles with a graphic character. This device is not only useful to the readers but to anyone proofreading your pub-lications. The graphic element as-sures them that they have reached the end of the article and that no text is missing or located else-where in the publication. To add a graphic character, simply click an insertion point at the end of the ar-ticle and use the Symbol dialog box (see the tip on page 73). Or you can use the drawing tools to design and create your own shape (see page 88).

Editorial Decisions

Now that you have decided on the placement of the stories and graphics in the newsletter, you can begin to add the text. You can use several methods to make text fit in a publication:

Making text fit

- **Editing.** You can edit the text to fit it in the allotted space.

- **Multiple frames.** You can flow text from a frame on one page to a frame on another.

- **Fillers.** When an article does not occupy all the space you've allowed for it, you can fill gaps with visual elements.

As a demonstration, you are going to copy a paragraph from the brochure you created in Chapter 3 and repeatedly paste it throughout the newsletter. That way, you won't have to spend time entering pages of text. (Our purpose here is to show you how to deal with longer stories, not to teach you how to type!)

Copyfitting by Editing

In this section, we'll give you a few editorial pointers for copyfitting text. First add more text to the Turtle Mountains article so that you can experiment:

1. Save Newsletter and open Brochure.

2. Select the fossil dig tours paragraph in the left panel of the first page by clicking its frame and pressing Ctrl+A. Then click the Copy button.

3. Reopen Newsletter, press F9 to zoom to 100%, and move to the bottom of the first page.

4. Click the text frame of the Turtle Mountains article, and with all the text selected, click the Paste button to replace the placeholder text by pasting in the brochure paragraph.

Changing line spacing

5. To match the formatting of the other newsletter paragraphs, select the newly inserted paragraph and choose Line Spacing from the Format menu to display the dialog box shown earlier on page 64. Enter *1.17* as the Between Lines setting and *6* as the After Paragraphs setting and click OK.

6. Click a blank area of the page to see these results:

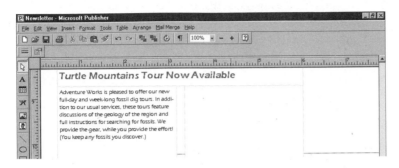

7. Reselect the new paragraph and click the Copy button to copy the paragraph with the correct formatting.

8. Press End to move the insertion point to the end of the selected paragraph, press Enter, and then click the Paste button.

9. Press Enter and click the Paste button again to insert the paragraph a third time. Publisher displays this message box:

10. You'll learn how to flow text from frame to frame in the next section, so click No to return to the story, which now has a Text In Overflow indicator.

To fit text in a frame, you can try eliminating extraneous words to decrease the number of lines or adding words to increase the number of lines. Depending on the type of text you are dealing with and whether you have the authority to make changes to it, you might consider the following:

- **Active vs. passive.** Active sentences are usually shorter than passive ones. For example, *We provide the gear* is one word shorter than *The gear will be provided*.

- **Words vs. phrases.** You can often expand words into phrases or contract phrases into words. For example, *the geology of the region* is two words longer than *the region's geology*.

Inserting and deleting pages

To insert new pages in a one-page publication, choose Page from the Insert menu. In the Insert Page dialog box, designate how many pages you want to insert and whether they should appear before or after the existing page. You can also set options that allow you to insert a blank page, a page with one text frame that takes up the whole page, or a page that duplicates all objects on an existing page of the publication. To insert new pages in a multi-page publication, you must insert two-page spreads. Choose Page from the Insert menu to display a different Insert Page dialog box. Then designate what you want to appear on the left and right pages by selecting options from drop-down lists. (You can add calendars and forms, for example.) To delete a page, move to the page, choose Delete Page from the Edit menu, and click Yes to confirm the action.

- **Simple vs. compound structures.** You can often insert or delete adjectives or adverbs without changing meaning, and you can substitute shorter or longer words or interchange simple and compound verbs. For example, *Adventure Works is very pleased to be able to offer our exciting new full-day and week-long fossil dig tours* is five words longer than the equivalent sentence in the newsletter.

With the Turtle Mountains story, you can either leave the text in the overflow area or delete all but the first sentence of the third paragraph to make the text fit in its frame.

Flowing Text from Frame to Frame

When placing longer articles in a multi-page publication, you will often need to start on one page and continue on another. Because all text must be contained in a frame, you need to be able to tell Publisher which frame to continue the text in. When you use the Newsletter Wizard, the process is fairly simple because Publisher has already designated the connected frames. (For other publications, you will need to manually connect the appropriate frames; see the adjacent tip.) To add the text for the fossil dig story on page 1 and continue the story on page 3 of the newsletter, follow these steps:

1. Scroll page 1 until the Fossil Dig story comes into view, select its placeholder text, and press Delete.

2. Click the Paste button to insert the paragraph you copied from the Turtle Mountains story, and then press Enter. Repeat this step four more times.

3. When Publisher displays the message box shown on the previous page, click Yes. Publisher jumps to the next available text frame (in this case, the Adventure Works Souvenirs article on page 2) and asks if this is where you want to autoflow the text.

4. Click No. Publisher moves on to the next story and displays the message box again.

5. Click No two more times. When Publisher reaches the article on page 3 (the continuation of the fossil dig story), click Yes. Publisher inserts the remaining text of the paragraph, as shown at the top of the facing page.

Connecting text frames

To continue a story in an empty text frame that you have created, first click the frame that already contains the story and then choose Connect Text Frames from the Tools menu to display the Connect Frames toolbar. Click the Connect Text Frames button. When the mouse pointer changes to a pitcher, click the empty text frame to "pour" the story into that frame. To disconnect two text frames, click the first frame and then click the Disconnect Text Frames button on the Connect Frames toolbar. The other frame is then removed from the chain, and the remaining text of the story is placed back in the text overflow area until you pour it somewhere else or make the first frame big enough to display it all.

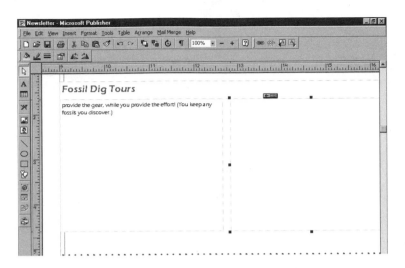

6. Click an insertion point at the end of the paragraph, press Enter, and then paste the paragraph again. Repeat this step three more times to finish up the story.

7. With the last frame of the article selected, click the Go To Previous Frame button to move to the frame to the left of the selected frame.

The Go To Previous Frame button

8. Click the Go To Previous Frame button again to move to the second frame of the story, which is on page 1 of the newsletter.

As you can see, Publisher recognizes that these frames are connected. To move forward one frame in the story, you can click the Go To Next Frame button.

The Go To Next Frame button

To let the reader know on which page the story continues or where the story began, you can add a *Continued On* or *Continued From* line to the article. Follow these steps:

Adding "continued on" lines

1. With the second frame of the Fossil Dig story selected on the first page of the newsletter, click the Text Frame Properties button on the Formatting toolbar to display the dialog box shown earlier on page 59.

2. In the Options section, click the Include "Continued On Page" check box to select it and click OK. The results are shown on the next page.

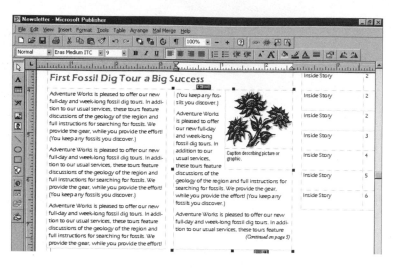

Notice that you don't have to enter a page number. Because the frames are connected, Publisher knows that the story continues on page 3. Also notice that by adding this line to the selected frame, you have bumped one line of text to page 3.

3. The second frame would look better with one more line to balance the two "columns," so make the frame a little larger to run back the displaced line of text.

Adding "continued from" lines

4. Click the Go To Next Frame button to move to page 3, click the Text Frame Properties button, click the Include "Continued From Page" check box, and click OK. This time, Publisher adds a line to the top of the selected frame, as shown here:

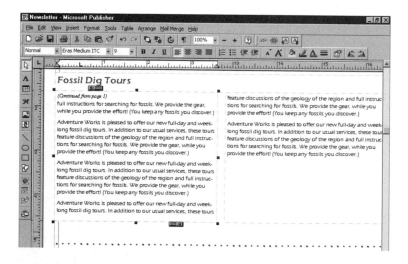

Now that you've finished the Fossil Dig Tours article, you need to add the same placeholder text for the remaining four articles before moving on to other elements of the newsletter. Follow these steps:

1. Scroll to the left until page 2 comes into view, and replace the text of the Adventure Works Souvenirs article with two copies of the brochure paragraph.

2. Move to the Sandy's Stories article and paste in three copies of the paragraph.

3. Next paste two copies of the paragraph in the Preserve Our National Parks article.

4. Move to page 4 and paste five copies of the paragraph in the final article of the newsletter.

5. Save your work.

Filling Blank Areas

After entering all the text of a longer publication, you can begin to juggle the other elements. In the publishing world, the blank areas of a page are known as *white space*. If you crowd too many different items of information together, your message can get lost, so a well-designed publication uses a certain amount of white space to visually separate the items. However, too much white space can make a publication look empty, boring, unbalanced, or all three! Let's take a closer look at each page of the newsletter and add visual elements where they will enhance its overall appearance:

White space

1. Move to page 1 and change the zoom setting to 33% so that you can see the entire page at a glance. The first two columns are filled with text but the last column contains too much white space.

2. Press F9, scroll to the top of the page, and verify that the rulers are turned on.

3. Click the Clip Gallery Tool button on the Objects toolbar, and draw a frame 1¼ inches high and 1¾ inches wide below the Volume 1 frame.

The Clip Gallery Tool button

4. When the Clip Gallery dialog box appears, search for the desert graphic you used earlier (see page 84). Then click it and click the Insert Clip button to the add the graphic to page 1. Close the Clip Gallery.

5. If necessary, use the Nudge command on the Arrange menu (see page 85) to fine-tune the placement of the graphic so that it aligns with the text in the frames above and below it.

6. Next replace the graphic adjacent to the Fossil Dig Tour article with the bone picture from the brochure. Reposition and resize the graphic as necessary.

7. Replace the caption below the graphic with *Who knows...you might find the remains of a dinosaur!* Then click the Center button on the Formatting toolbar to center the caption under the graphic. Here are the results:

Let's fill the white space at the bottom of the right column:

Inserting attention-getters

1. Scroll to the bottom right corner of page 1. Click the Design Gallery Object button on the Objects toolbar, select the Attention Getters category, and double-click Explosion Attention Getter to insert it on page 1.

2. Move the object into the white space to the right of the Turtle Mountains story and click outside the object to deselect it.

3. Now select the 2 For 1 text frame by clicking its border, press Ctrl+A to highlight all the text, and type *New!*.

4. Next click the object outside the text frame, and click the Custom Rotate button on the Standard toolbar to display the dialog box shown earlier on page 90. Enter *345* in the Angle edit box and click Close.

5. Click the Fill Color button and change the object's color (we chose gold).

6. Finally, resize the object until it looks something like the one shown here:

This Design Gallery object helps draw the reader's attention to a story that might otherwise get lost at the bottom of the page. The object's color is subdued, but because it is not immediately surrounded by any other object, it pops out on the page.

Now let's move on to the second page of the newsletter:

1. Move to pages 2 and 3, change the zoom setting to 33%, and scroll the window so that you can see the two-page spread. The most glaring area of white space is next to the first article, but this space is reserved for a table, which will balance nicely with the form at the bottom of page 3. The items on page 2 that need your attention are the boxed quote and the graphic that accompanies the last article.

2. Press F9, move to the quote frame on page 2, select the placeholder text, and type *"The archaeology of the Mojave Desert has always been a special interest of mine." Dinah Soar, Adventure Works guide.* (A quote frame is a good way to fill

Creating a quote box from
scratch

white space and draw the eye toward a story. To create one
from scratch, you can use objects in the Pull Quotes category
in the Design Gallery.)

3. Now scroll to the National Parks article on page 2, double-click
the placeholder graphic to open the Clip Gallery, and select a
suitable replacement. (We used the desert scene again.) Click
Insert Clip, and then close the Clip Gallery.

4. Delete the new graphic's caption text. (You don't need to delete the frame.)

5. Resize the bottom of the article's first frame to push more text
to the second frame. Then move and resize the graphic until it
balances with the quote box of the preceding article, like this:

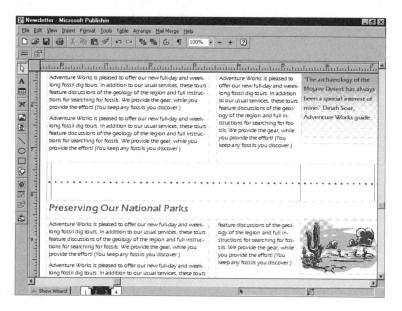

As you can see, you can experiment with the size of text
frames and objects to force text to rewrap, thereby filling
white space and balancing the page.

6. On page 3, replace the graphic to the right of the form with
something appropriate.

You're going to deal with the form at the bottom of page 3
later. For now, turn your attention to page 4 where you need
to update the logo. Follow the steps on the facing page.

1. Move to page 4 and scroll to the top of the page.

2. Select the Organization Name frame and delete it. Then select the logo and delete it.

3. Save Newsletter and open Brochure.

Recycling a logo

4. Copy the logo, reopen Newsletter, and paste the logo on page 4.

5. Move the logo to the upper left corner and then resize it until its frame is the same width as the one below it and all its text is visible.

6. Move to the oval object advertising the Web address and replace the text with *Check out our Web site at www.adworks.tld.*

7. Move the object down so that its information does not get lost below the address and phone frames.

8. Finally, replace the graphic in the bottom right corner of the page with a graphic that fits the adjacent article. Then position and size the graphic so that the text rewraps in a skinny column to its left. The results are shown here at 40%:

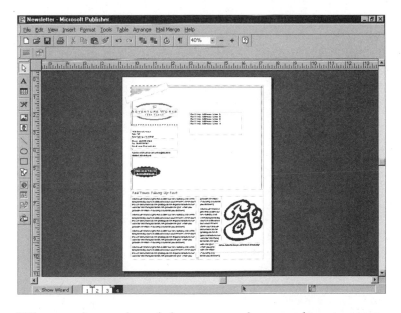

When you're ready, rejoin us as we show you how to create a table.

Creating Tables from Scratch

In Chapter 3, you filled in a table that Publisher had added to the brochure to create a price list. For times when you need to create tables from scratch, you draw a table frame and enter the necessary settings in a dialog box. To demonstrate how easy the process is, we'll show you how to create a table that lists the merchandise sold by Adventure Works as souvenirs:

1. Move to page 2, select the empty text frame to the right of the Adventure Works Souvenirs article, and press Delete.

The Table Frame Tool button

2. Press F9, and click the Table Frame Tool button on the Objects toolbar. Move the cross-hair pointer over the newsletter, and drag a frame in the empty area to the right of the Adventure Works Souvenirs article. When you release the mouse button, Publisher displays this dialog box:

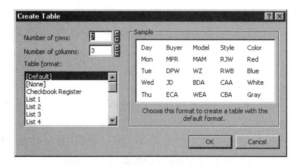

Working with tabs

Many tables are simple tabular lists that align information in columns. To use tabs, enter the text of the list and press the Tab key when you want to move to a different column. The insertion point jumps to a position that corresponds to that of the next tab setting. By default, Publisher sets tabs at every half inch. To adjust the position of the default tabs, choose Tabs from the Format menu and change the Default Tab Stops setting. To set a custom tab using this dialog box, enter the tab's position in the Tab Stop Position edit box and click Set. Publisher adds the tab to the Tab Stop Position list below the edit box. You can also specify how the text should be aligned at the tab and whether the tabs should have leaders. For example, if you create a table of contents for a report, you might want to set a Right tab with dot leaders to draw your readers' eyes from a heading across the page to a page number. You can also use the ruler to set custom tabs. First select the paragraphs that will contain the tabs and then, on the horizontal ruler, click where you want the tab to appear. Publisher places a left-aligned tab marker on the ruler. To adjust the tab's position, drag the marker to the left or right. To set a tab with different alignment, click the Tab button between the rulers until it displays an icon for the alignment you want and then click a location for the custom tab. (An *L* is a left-aligned tab, an upside-down *T* is a centered tab, a backwards *L* is a right-aligned tab, and an upside-down *T* with a period is a decimal-aligned tab.) When you set a custom tab, Publisher removes all the default tabs to the left of the new tab but retains the default tabs to the right.

3. Change the Number Of Rows setting to *4* and the Number Of Columns setting to *2*, and then click OK. The table looks something like this:

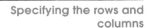

Specifying the rows and columns

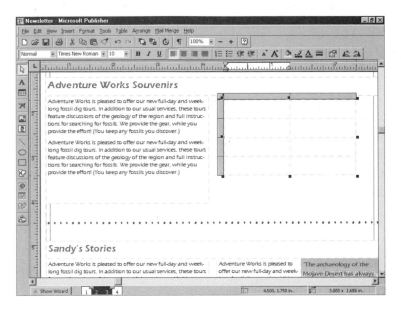

4. In the first cell, type *Baseball Caps*, press Tab to move to the next cell, type *$15.00*, and then press Tab to move to the next row.

5. Next type the entries shown below, pressing Tab to move from cell to cell:

100% Cotton T-Shirts	*$20.00*
100% Cotton Sweatshirts	*$35.00*
Tour Videos	*$45.00*

Looking over the table, you can see one or two changes that would make it more effective. We discuss ways to edit tables in the next section.

Changing Column Width and Row Height

You can change the default column widths and row heights in a table to make its information easier to read. Try this:

1. With the insertion point in the table, point to the gray bar above the second column. When the pointer turns into a pointing hand, click once to select the column.

Importing table data from another source

To import tabular data from another program into a Publisher table, first open the file in the program in which you originally entered the data and copy it. Next open Publisher. If you are copying the tabular data into an existing blank Publisher table, click an insertion point in the blank table. Choose Paste Special from the Edit menu, select the Table Cells With Cell Formatting option from the Paste Special dialog box, and click OK. To insert a new table with the copied text on the active page of a publication, choose Paste Special and click the New Table option. Then click yes in the message box that appears.

2. Move the pointer to the right end of the selected column's gray bar. When the word *ADJUST* appears below a two-headed pointer, drag to the left until the column is just wide enough to display its text.

You can also adjust the size of more than one row or column at a time, like this:

Adjusting multiple rows/ columns simultaneously

1. Choose Select and then Table from the Table menu to select the entire table.

2. On the gray bar to the left of the table, point to the boundary between any two rows and drag up until the dotted line that shows what the new height will be is where you want it. Click away from the table to view these results:

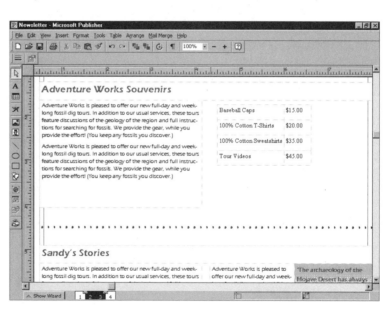

The Fill command

To copy the contents of one cell to the cells below or to the right of it, select the cell you want to copy and all cells you want its contents copied to. Then choose either Fill Down or Fill Right from the Table menu. Publisher copies the contents of the cell you first selected to the remaining cells in the selection.

Adding a Title

Suppose you want to add a row above the table for a title. The first step is to insert a new row, like this:

1. Click an insertion point anywhere in the first row of the table.

2. Choose Insert Rows Or Columns from the Table menu to display the dialog box shown at the top of the facing page.

3. With Rows selected in the Insert section and the Number Of Rows setting at *1*, click Before Selected Cells in the Options section. Then click OK to insert a new row above the row containing the insertion point.

4. Now enter the title. Click an insertion point in the first cell in the top row and type *Merchandise Price List*.

Next you need to join the cells of the new row to create one large cell. Then you can center the table's title above the columns. Joining cells is a simple one-step procedure:

1. Click the gray bar to the left of the top row to select the row, and choose Merge Cells from the Table menu. Publisher combines the two cells of the row into one large cell that spans the table. The results are shown here:

Merging cells

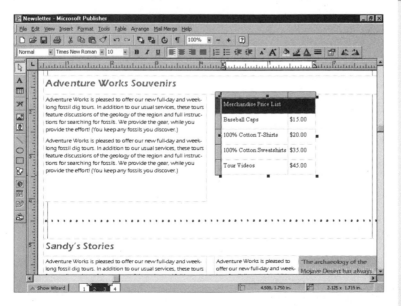

Rearranging tables

To rearrange a table, select the row or column you want to move and click the Cut button. Click an insertion point in the row above which or the column to the left of which you want the cut information to appear and choose Insert Rows Or Columns from the Table menu. Select the appropriate options and click OK. Then with the new row or column selected, click the Paste button, and click Yes in the message box to paste in the text. Finally, select the empty row or column and delete it by choosing the appropriate command from the Table menu.

Formatting Tables

Having made all the necessary structural changes to the table, let's add some finishing touches. First you need to format the title. Follow these steps:

Centering cell entries

1. With the title of the table selected, click the Center button to center the text in the merged cell.

2. Now click the Font Color button and change the color to blue. Then change the font to Eras Demi ITC and the size to 12.

3. Select the four rows below the title by dragging down the gray bar to the left of the rows. Then change the font to Eras Medium ITC and the size to 9.

4. Click outside the table to see the results so far:

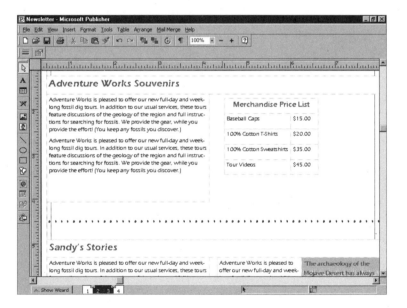

Now you're ready to add gridlines and a border:

Adding gridlines and a border

1. Click an insertion point anywhere in the table and point to the gray box at the intersection of the row and column bars. When the pointer changes to a white hand, click to select the entire table.

2. Click the Line/Border Style button on the Formatting toolbar and then choose More Styles to display the dialog box shown earlier on page 54.

3. In the Preset section, select Grid to add a border and gridlines to the table. (To add only a border, select the Box option.)

4. Change the Color setting to blue and the Width setting to 2 pt, and then click OK.

5. Select the first row of the table (which contains the table's title), click the Fill Color button on the Formatting toolbar, and select gold.

Filling cells with color

6. Next click away from the title to see the results. Adjust the position of the table frame and the width of the columns as necessary to make your table look something like the one shown here:

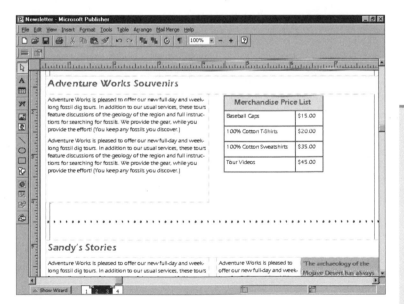

Table autoformats

An easy way to apply formatting to a table is to use Publisher's table autoformats. Click an insertion point anywhere in the table you want to format and choose Table AutoFormat from the Table menu. In the Auto Format dialog box, you can select from a variety of table styles. Click a name in the Table Format list to display a sample of the format in the Sample box. You can modify the style by clicking the Options button and making your selections in the lower portion of the dialog box. Click OK to complete the changes and you instantly have a great-looking table.

7. Save your work.

Page 1 of this publication features another table, which Publisher created to draw attention to the articles that appear on the inside of the newsletter. Let's quickly fill in this table now by following the steps on the next page.

1. Move to page 1 and then scroll the Inside This Issue table into view.

2. Replace the Inside Story placeholder text and the page numbers with the following:

   Adventure Works Souvenirs   2
   Sandy's Stories   2
   Preserving Our National Parks   2
   Tour Sign-up Form   3
   Fall Tours Filling Up Fast   4

3. Select the remaining two rows and then choose Delete Rows from the Table menu.

4. Click an insertion point in front of the *S* in *Souvenirs* and press Shift+Enter to rebreak the line. Repeat this step to move *National* to the second line in the third row and to move *Up* to the second line in the fifth row. Here are the results:

Adding graphs

Publisher works with the Microsoft Graph program, which you use to create graphs and charts. To start Graph, choose Object from the Insert menu, select Microsoft Graph 2000 Chart from the Object Type list, and click OK. Publisher loads Graph and displays both a datasheet and a graph it has plotted from the datasheet's data. (Graph's menu bar and toolbars replace Publisher's at the top of the window.) Use the datasheet to enter your data and watch as Graph updates the plotted graph. You can then format the graph by changing the graph type, changing colors, and adding other elements such as titles and labels. For more information on using Graph, check Graph's Help menu. To return to your publication, click anywhere outside the graph frame. You can then move, resize, and format the frame just as you would any other Publisher frame.

Working with Forms

When you first created the newsletter on page 96, you told Publisher to include a sign-up form on page 3 of the publication. Publisher has several form types, each of which you can use as an element of a publication or as its own publication. (If you are using Publisher to create a Web site, you can also insert a form on a Web page; see the tip on page 169.) Each type consists of a set of text frames that may also include one or more tables. As a demonstration, let's fill in the information needed for a tour sign-up form:

1. Move to page 3 of the newsletter and change the zoom setting to 150% so that you can see the text better. Then scroll the form into view.

Customizing forms

2. Replace the Sign-Up Form Title placeholder with *Jeep Tour Sign-Up Form*.

3. Change the heading of the middle column of the table below the title from *Time* to *Date*. Then delete all the placeholder numbers in the Date column.

4. In the first *Type the event* box, enter the following: *Two-Hour Mojave Desert Highlights Tour*.

5. Next select the price and type *$45.00*.

6. Repeat steps 4 and 5, entering the information shown here:

Half-Day Joshua Tree National Park Tour	*$55.00*
Half-Day Old Woman Mountains Tour	*$65.00*
Half-Day Turtle Mountains Tour	*$65.00*
Full-Day Providence Mountains Tour	*$95.00*
Week-Long Death Valley National Park Tour	*$495.00*

The last tour description is too long to fit in its cell, but type the entire entry anyway; you'll fix the cell width in a moment.

Adding a form to an existing publication

If you are already working on a publication and want to add a form to it, you can do so easily by using the Design Gallery. Click the Design Gallery Object button on the Objects toolbar and then click the Reply Forms category. Here, you can select from several styles for order forms, response forms, and sign-up forms. When you find one you like, simply double-click it to insert it in your publication. Then customize it as described above. You can then format it, size it, and reposition it anywhere in your publication using the techniques you have learned for working with text and frames.

Other available forms

If you want to create a business form using Publisher, check out the Business Forms category in the Catalog dialog box before you try to create one from scratch. You can select from a variety of common forms, such as expense reports, fax cover sheets, invoices, and purchase orders.

Customizing Forms

When Publisher adds a form to one of your publications, the program takes care of most of the details. However, you will often need to customize the form to meet your specific needs. For this example, you need to widen the column containing the tour descriptions so that they all fit, and you need to add a row for another tour. You can speed up these processes by grouping objects so that you can manipulate them together. Follow these steps:

Grouping objects

1. Click the Date frame to select it, hold down the Shift key, and click the Price frame. Then, still holding down the Shift key, click each of the frames in the Date and Price columns, including the Subtotal, Tax, and Total frames. Publisher selects all the frames, surrounding them with a blue border and handles, as shown here:

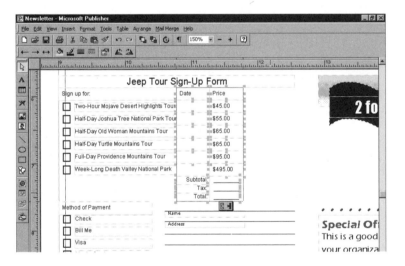

2. Click the Group Objects button to group the frames together. Now Publisher surrounds the entire group with a single border and set of handles.

Moving grouped objects

3. Point to the top border, and when the moving van appears, move the grouped objects to the right about ¼ inch.

4. Select the Sign Up For frame, hold down the Shift key, add all the tour description frames to the selection, and then click the Group Objects button.

5. Next widen the grouped object by dragging the right middle handle until it touches the left side of the Date column, as shown here:

Sizing grouped objects

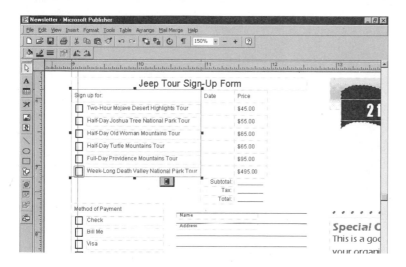

Now you're ready to add a row for the last tour description, but first you need to move the payment and address sections of the form down to make room for the new row. Again, you'll group the sections together, but this time using a different method. Follow these steps:

1. Scroll down the page and select the Adventure Works frame below the form. Then resize the frame so that it is just high enough to fit its text, by dragging the top middle handle downward.

2. To group the payment and address information together for one easy move, first click the Pointer Tool button on the Objects toolbar (even though it is already active). Point above and to the left of the Method Of Payment frame. Check that there is no MOVE box attached to the pointer. Then hold down the left mouse button, and drag until the pointer is below and to the right of the Expiration date frame. As you drag, Publisher draws a rectangle around all the frames you want to select. When you release the mouse button, Publisher selects all the frames inside the selection rectangle and surrounds them with a blue border and sets of handles, as shown on the next page.

The Pointer Tool button

3. Click the Group Objects button to group the items together, and then move the grouped object down until it sits just above the Adventure Works frame.

4. Now select the Date/Price grouped object, and click the Ungroup Objects button. Then do the same thing for the Sign Up For grouped object.

5. Group the Subtotal, Tax, and Total frames and move them down to make room for the new row. (You may have to increase the zoom setting to be able to select all the frames.)

Copying a row

6. Hold down the Shift key and select the last tour description and its date and price frames.

7. Click the Copy button to copy the selection and then click the Paste button.

8. Move the copy of the row so that it sits below the preceding row and aligns with the other frames. Then if necessary, adjust the position of the Subtotal grouped object.

9. In the copied tour description frame, replace the description with *Week-Long Mojave Desert Fossil Dig Tour* and the price text with *$610.00*. Here are the results at 100%:

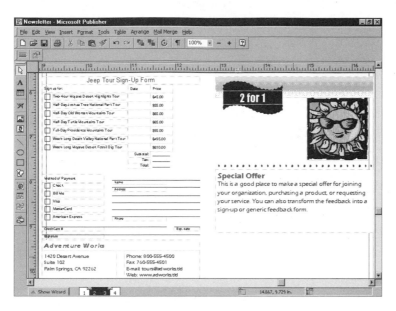

10. To finish up this section, enter the following text beneath the Special Offer heading to the right of the form:

    Buy two tickets for our Full-Day Providence Mountains Tour between now and June 12, 2000, and pay for only one ($95). Hurry to book your tour now. Space is limited or is already sold out for some dates.

11. To see a printout of the newsletter, click the Print button. Then save and close the publication.

    You should now have a good understanding of what is involved in designing and creating longer, more complex publications. If you use the concepts we have introduced here along with Publisher's wizards, you'll have no trouble developing professional-looking printed materials. Once you feel comfortable with the program, you can experiment on your own. (Often the most attention-grabbing designs break all the rules!)

5 Creating a Custom Template

You learn how to design a template as you create a press release from scratch. We show you how to add items to the background so that they can be repeated on every page, and how to develop a custom color scheme. Finally, you create a publication based on your template.

If your organization has already developed a promotional image, you can use the skills you acquire in this chapter to ensure that the publications you produce coordinate with other promotional materials.

Publication created and concepts covered:

Use elements from the Design Gallery, discarding parts you don't want

Place elements on the background layer so that they appear on all pages

Rotate text to create interesting visual effects

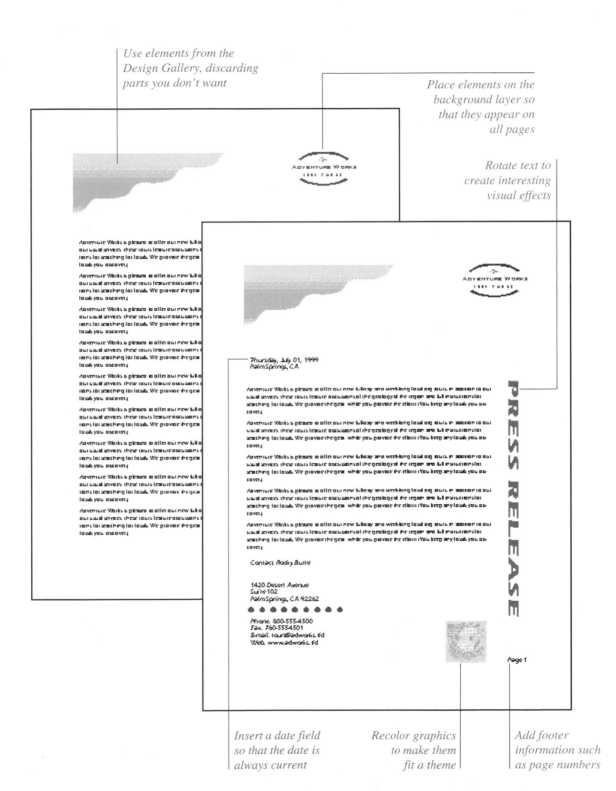

Insert a date field so that the date is always current

Recolor graphics to make them fit a theme

Add footer information such as page numbers

As you know, Publisher provides a wide variety of design templates to choose from, but you aren't limited to those templates. You can create your own, either by modifying an existing template or by designing a new one from scratch. You may think now that you will never need or want to create your own design template, but bear in mind that many organizations use Publisher to create their marketing materials. There is always the possibility that a competitor will wind up selecting the same Publisher-designed template and the same color scheme as you!

In this chapter, we show you how to create a press release template that uses your choice of fonts, graphics, color scheme, and so on. You then create a new publication based on the custom template so that you can see your design in action. With the skills you learn here, you will be able to experiment with creating your own designs or modifying existing ones to get just the effect you want.

Creating a Publication Template

Before you start work on a new template, you need to ask yourself some simple questions like these:

- **The design.** What elements do you want to include?
- **The look.** Should it be formal or informal?
- **The message.** What do you want to convey?

Design consistency

For demonstration purposes, suppose you want to create a template that can be used for the press releases that Adventure Works sends out periodically to travel agencies and local hotels. In previous chapters, you used the Waves design template and the Tropics color scheme. For the press releases, you still want to use elements of the Waves design to tie them in with other Adventure Works promotional materials. Because Adventure Works is in the recreation business, you want an informal look, which can also be achieved with the Waves design template. However, you want the press releases to catch the eye of busy travel and hospitality agents, so the color scheme needs to be more lively.

Having decided on the direction you want to take, follow the steps below to open a blank publication:

1. Start Publisher, and when the Catalog dialog box appears, click the Blank Publications tab to display the layout options shown here:

Opening a blank publication

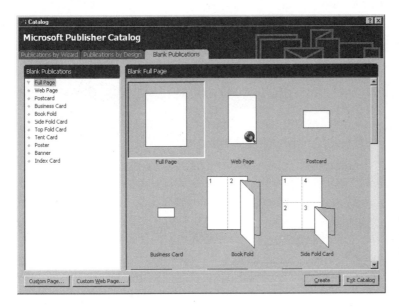

2. Double-click the Full Page option to display a blank, 8½-by-11-inch page in Publisher's window, and then click the Hide Wizard button.

Saving a Custom Template

You have quite a bit of design work to do, but before you get started, you should save the page as a template to safeguard your changes. Publisher designates a folder on your hard drive as the default location for templates. If you store your templates here, you can click the Templates button at the bottom of the Catalog dialog box to display an Open Template dialog box that lists the names of the templates in the default location. You can store templates in a different location, but because Publisher's default setup makes it easy to create new documents based on your custom templates, we recommend that you stick with the default. Follow the steps on the next page to save the template.

Other blank publication types

On the Blank Publications tab of the Catalog dialog box, you can choose from several blank publication types. These types include specifications for the size of the page and the way the publication is folded. If none of these types fit your needs, click the Custom Page button at the bottom of the tab or click the Custom Web Page button if you are creating a Web page from scratch. Publisher then displays the Page Setup dialog box, where you can select your layout style, change the dimensions, and select the orientation (portrait or landscape). When you finish, click OK to display the new publication. If you need to make further page setup modifications, choose Page Setup from the File menu to redisplay the dialog box.

Saving a publication
as a template

1. Choose Save As from the File menu. In the Save As dialog box, change the Save As Type setting to Publisher Template. Publisher immediately moves to the C:\Windows\Application Data\Microsoft\Templates folder on your hard drive and displays Templates in the Save In box.

2. In the File Name edit box, type *Press Release* as the name of the custom template, and click Save.

   As with any Publisher file, from now on you can simply click the Save button to save any changes you make to the new template. (Although we don't always explicitly tell you to, you should save your work often.)

Adding Design Elements

A blank page is a bit intimidating. Where do you begin? Well, the simplest thing to do is to look for design elements that resemble those you have in mind, bring them into your template, and then customize them. Let's use this technique to insert the wave design element in the press release. Follow these steps:

Using pre-defined elements

1. Click the Design Gallery Object button on the Objects toolbar. With the Mastheads category selected, scroll to the bottom of the Mastheads pane, and select Waves Masthead. Then click the Insert Object button. Publisher places the masthead in a frame on the blank page.

2. You want only the wave pattern of the masthead, not the text frames, so first choose Ungroup Objects from the expanded Arrange menu. Click Yes in the message box to ungroup the objects in the masthead.

3. Click outside the masthead to deselect all the frames, and change the zoom setting to 100%.

4. Next right-click the Newsletter Title frame and choose Delete Object from the shortcut menu. Then repeat this step to remove the Newsletter Date frame, the Adventure Works frame and its oval background, the Volume 1 frame, and also the arrow.

5. Move the yellow wave shape (it is composed of two frames) to the top left corner of the page, until it is top- and left-aligned with the pink layout guides, as shown here:

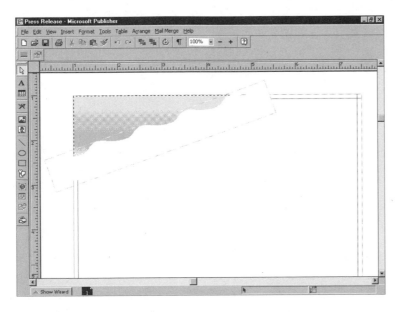

Now you need to add more items to the template, such as the Adventure Works logo, address and phone information, and a banner. Some of these elements will appear on the left side of the page and others will appear on the right, and you will be able to position them more easily if you use column guides. Let's display these now before you go any further with the press release's contents:

1. Choose Layout Guides from the Arrange menu to display the dialog box shown on the following page.

Displaying column guides

More layout guide options

In the Layout Guides dialog box, you can set the margin guides for all four sides of a page. (Note that these settings determine the position of the guides, not the position of the margins themselves.) You can also add row grid guides by entering a number in the Rows edit box in the Grid Guides section of the dialog box. If your publication has facing pages and you want to adjust the inside and outside margins of the pages, click the Create Two Backgrounds With Mirrored Guides check box. (When you click this check box, you also tell Publisher to create a left background for left pages and a right background for right pages. See the tip on page 134 for more information about backgrounds.) As you make adjustments to the layout guides, Publisher displays a sample of the results in the adjacent Preview box. When you're ready, click OK to implement the changes.

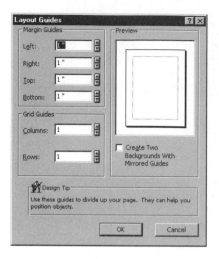

2. In the Grid Guides section, change the Columns setting to *3* and click OK. At 33%, the page now looks like this:

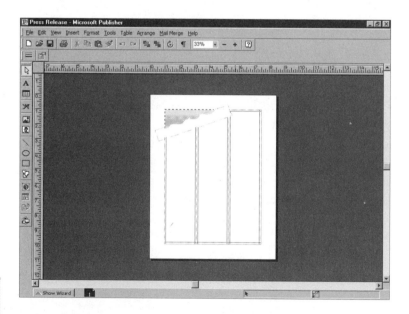

Remember, these layout guides do not appear on the page and, unlike frames, do not restrict where you can place template elements. They serve as guides to align items on the page.

Now let's add a few more items to the template:

1. Copy and paste the logo from Brochure into the template. (To reopen the template, simply choose the filename from the bottom of the File menu.)

Opening templates

If you have to quit Publisher in the middle of designing a template, you can easily return to the template by first clicking the Open button, navigating to the C:\Windows\Application Data\ Microsoft\Templates folder, and double-clicking the name of the template.

2. If necessary, change the zoom setting to 100%. Then move the logo to the top right corner.

3. Now click the Text Frame Tool button on the Objects toolbar and draw a frame anywhere on the page.

4. Type *PRESS RELEASE* and change the font to Eras Bold ITC and the size to 24.

5. With the text still selected, choose Character Spacing from the Format menu to display this dialog box:

Stretching text

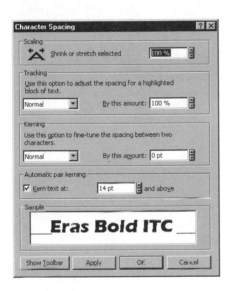

6. In the Scaling section, change the Shrink Or Stretch Selected setting to 200% and click OK. (For more information on this dialog box, see the tip on page 52.)

7. Next resize the frame until all of the text is displayed on just one line.

8. To make the text run down the right side of the page, click the Rotate Right button on the Formatting toolbar. Publisher rotates the frame 90 degrees to the right.

The Rotate Right button

9. Zoom to 50%, and then move the frame to the right side of the page so that it sits a couple of inches below the logo and is aligned with the blue layout guide on the right. The results are shown on the next page.

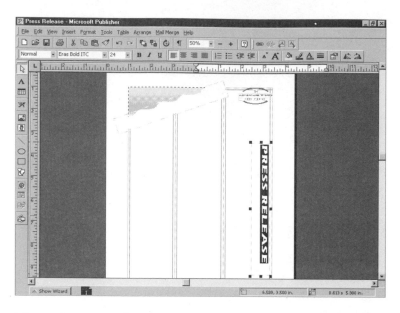

That takes care of the right column. Now let's put the company's address and contact information in the left column. Follow these steps:

1. First press F9 to zoom to 100%, and then draw a text frame in the left column below the wave design element. (The frame should be as wide as the blue column layout guides and about ½ inch high.)

Inserting a date field

2. Choose Date And Time from the expanded Insert menu to display this dialog box:

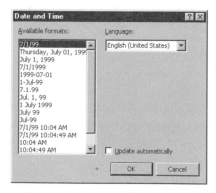

3. Select the option in the list that is the equivalent of *Thursday, July 01, 1999*, click the Update Automatically check box to

select it, and then click OK to insert the date in the frame. Now whenever you use this template, Publisher will automatically obtain the current date from your computer's built-in clock and display it in the press release in the selected format.

4. Press Enter to add a second line to the frame and then type *Palm Springs, CA*. Change the font of both lines of text to Eras Demi ITC.

5. Move to the bottom of the page and, at about the 7½-inch mark on the vertical ruler, draw a text frame the width of the blue layout guides and about ¼ inch high in the first column.

6. Type *Contact: Rocky Butte* and then change the font to Eras Demi ITC.

7. Use the Personal Information command on the Insert menu to insert a frame containing the company's address. Then move the frame about ¼ inch below the Contact line, change the font to Eras Demi ITC, and resize the frame so that it is the same width as the Contact frame and just high enough to hold the address.

Inserting items from the personal information set

8. Repeat the previous step to insert the phone/fax/e-mail information about ¼ inch below the address information.

To break up the monotony of all this text, let's add a row of dots between the address and phone information:

1. Click the Design Gallery Object button on the Objects toolbar, select the Dots category, and double-click Far Dots to insert a frame containing a row of dots.

Inserting a row of dots

2. Move and resize the frame until it looks like the one below:

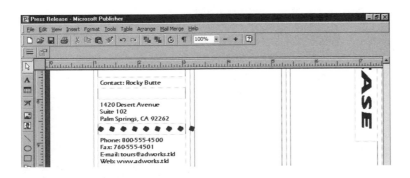

Adding Objects to the Background

So far, you have added elements that will appear only on the page they were added to. With some multi-page publications, you want certain elements to appear on every page. Examples include headers and footers (for page numbers or chapter names), graphics, or a logo. To repeat an element on every page, you add it to the background, which you can think of as a separate layer beneath each page (or foreground). In this section, you'll add a graphic and a footer to the background of the press release template so that when a press release is longer than one page, these elements appear automatically on every page. You will also move some items from the foreground to the background. First let's move to the background layer:

1. Zoom to 50% and scroll the window so that you can see pretty much the entire page.

Moving to the background layer →

2. Choose Go To Background from the expanded View menu. Because you added all the template's elements to its foreground, the background is blank.

Adding Graphics

Now let's add a graphic to the background of the template so that it will appear in the same place on every page. Graphics used in this way are sometimes called *watermarks* (see the tip below). Follow the steps on the facing page.

Watermarks

A watermark is a lightly shaded object appearing behind everything else on the page of a publication. First add the object that you want to use as the watermark to the background. Then choose Recolor Picture from the Format menu, select Fill Effects from the Color edit box, and select a light Tint/Shade option. Finally, select any objects in the foreground that obscure the watermark and press Ctrl+T to make them transparent.

Left and right backgrounds

If you are creating a publication with facing pages (such as a newsletter), you may want to have two backgrounds. To create two backgrounds, first choose Layout Guides from the Arrange menu, then select the Create Two Backgrounds With Mirrored Guides check box (see the tip on page 129 for more information about this dialog box), and click OK. Press Ctrl+M to move to the background. To switch between the left and right background pages, click the Left Background Page and Right Background Page buttons at the bottom of the publication window. To view both backgrounds at the same time, choose Two-Page Spread from the View menu. You can then add items to the background pages as usual. If you want an object to appear on both backgrounds, add the object to one page and then copy and paste it to the other page. You can then position the object so that it mirrors the one on the other page.

1. With the background displayed, click the Clip Gallery Tool button on the Objects toolbar and draw a frame in the bottom left corner of the right column.

2. In the Clip Gallery, find and insert the first sun graphic in the Weather category. (See page 80 if you need more help with this feature.)

3. To see the graphic's position in relation to items on the foreground, press Ctrl+M to activate the foreground layer. The results are shown below. (If your graphic needs some adjustment, press Ctrl+M to return to the background, resize and move the graphic as necessary, and press Ctrl+M again.)

Switching between foreground and background

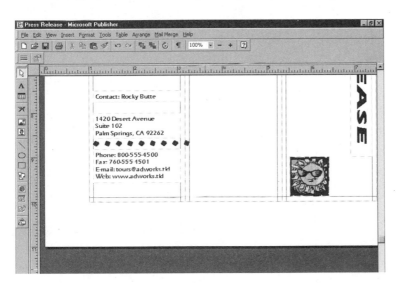

Adding background colors and textures

If your publication will be printed in color, you can add color or textured patterns to the background of your pages. To add the same background color or texture to every page of your publication, first move to the background layer. To make the background take up the entire page, draw a frame that is the same size as the margin guides. With the frame selected, click the Fill Color button on the Formatting toolbar. Select a color as usual or click Fill Effects to add tints/shades, patterns, or gradients. For graphic backgrounds, draw a clip art frame and select the Backgrounds category in the Clip Gallery window. Here, you can select from several graphic patterns appropriate for flyers or invitations. When you return to the foreground, select any objects that obscure the background color or graphic and press Ctrl+T to make them transparent so that your background shows through all frames properly. To add a background color or texture to just one page, draw a frame on the foreground and add the background as described above. Then click the Send To Back button on the Standard toolbar to move the background layer behind any other objects on the page. (See the tip on page 138 for more information about layering objects.)

Adding Headers and Footers

For publications that are longer than one page, you'll usually want to add information at the top or bottom of every page, such as the page number, date, or title of the publication. The information that appears at the top is called a header, and the information that appears at the bottom is called a footer. You add a header or footer in Publisher by drawing a text frame on the background layer and then entering and formatting text as usual. (You can create a header or footer for left pages and a different one for right pages; see the tip on page 134 for more information.) For the press release template, you want to add a page number that will appear in the bottom right corner of every page. Follow these steps:

1. Switch to the background and, if necessary, scroll the bottom right corner of the page into view.

2. Next draw a small text frame just to the right of the sun graphic.

Adding page numbers → 3. Type *Page* and a space, and then choose Page Numbers from the Insert menu. Publisher adds a pound sign (#) to indicate that the program will automatically insert the correct page number on every page of the publication.

4. Select the text (including the # sign) and then change the font to Eras Demi ITC.

The Align Right button → 5. Click the Align Right button to align the text along the right margin of the text frame.

6. Move and resize the frame as necessary to show all its text and bottom-align it with the sun graphic.

Hiding a header or footer on the first page

If you have added a header or footer to the background of a publication but don't want it displayed on the first page (or some other page), you can hide it. First move to page 1 of your publication and verify that you are on the foreground. If the header or footer is the only object on the background, choose Ignore Background from the View menu to turn off the background for that particular page. If there are other objects on the background that you do want displayed on the first page, draw a text frame on the foreground that is just large enough to cover the header or footer frame. When you print your publication, the empty text frame will "white out" the header or footer on the first page.

7. Switch to the foreground to display the results, as shown here:

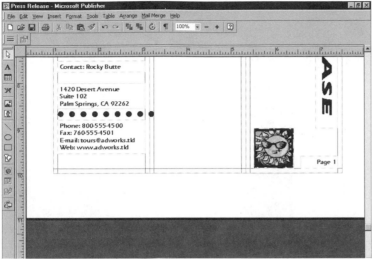

8. If necessary, return to the background to fine-tune the placement and size of the footer.

Moving Objects to the Background

What if you decide you want to move certain elements that are currently on the foreground layer to the background layer so that they too appear on every page of a publication? The process couldn't be easier. Let's say you've decided you want the wave design and the logo to appear on every page of the press release template. Follow these steps:

1. On the foreground, click the wave object once to select it.

2. Next choose Send To Background from the expanded Arrange menu, and then click OK to acknowledge the message that the move has taken place.

3. Press Ctrl+M to verify the move and then press Ctrl+M again to return to the foreground.

4. Repeat steps 1 through 3 to move the logo to the background. Then switch to the background and change the zoom setting to Whole Page to view the results, which are shown on the next page.

More about page numbers

If you want to add a page number to only one page in a publication, simply draw a text frame on the foreground and then use the Page Numbers command on the Insert menu as usual. To start a publication with a page number other than 1, choose Options from the Tools menu, enter the number you want in the Start Publication With Page edit box on the General tab, and click OK. To hide the page number on the first page or on a different page of a publication, use the method described in the tip on the facing page for hiding headers or footers.

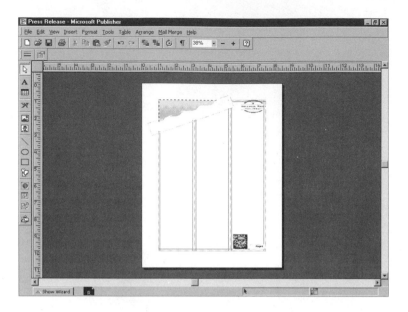

Well, that takes care of all the elements you want on the press release template. Now you need to make some decisions about a color scheme.

Creating a Custom Color Scheme

Throughout this book, you have used one of Publisher's predefined color schemes to save time and ensure a professional look. However, if you always use Publisher's color schemes, your publications may start to look "canned." As you become more comfortable using Publisher, you can experiment with your own color combinations to give your publications a unique look. In this section, you will first select a different predefined color scheme and then you'll customize it. Follow these steps:

1. First switch to the foreground.

2. Press F9 to zoom to 100%.

3. Next choose Color Scheme from the Format menu to display the Color Scheme dialog box shown at the top of the facing page.

Layering objects

On the previous page, you moved objects from the foreground layer to the background layer of the publication. However, if you have several objects that overlap each other on the same layer of a page, you can arrange them so that certain objects appear on top of or behind other objects. Choose the Bring To Front or Send To Back command from the Arrange menu to move the selected object to the top of the pile or send it to the bottom of the pile of overlapping objects. (The Bring To Front and Send To Back commands are also available as buttons on the Standard toolbar.) Move the selected object forward or backward one layer at a time by choosing the Send Forward or Send Backward command from the Arrange menu.

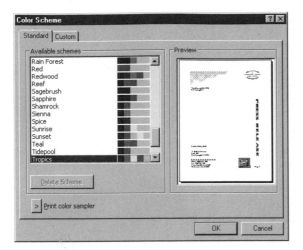

4. Scroll through the list, select Sunrise, and then click OK to see the results. This scheme includes some of the colors you want but you need to change some others.

5. Choose Color Scheme from the Format menu again and click the Custom tab to display these options:

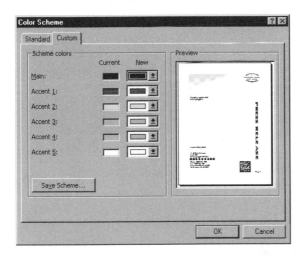

The Custom tab displays the main color as well as five accent colors. You can use the New box adjacent to each color to change the current color.

6. Click the arrow to the right of the New box in the Accent 1 row and click More Colors. You see the options shown on the following page.

The effect of color

If you plan to print in color, the colors you use in your publications are just as important as the fonts you use. Like fonts, different colors can send different messages to your audience. For example, "cool" colors such as green, blue, and violet are associated with oceans and pastoral settings and can imply peace and tranquillity. "Warm" colors such as red, orange, and yellow, on the other hand, are associated with fire and can imply aggression and intensity. You also need to be aware of these factors when selecting colors for a publication:

- Use cool colors, which tend to recede, as background colors. Use warm colors, which tend to advance, to call attention to specific items.

- Similarly, use muted colors in the background and bright colors to visually advance an element.

- Avoid placing red and green next to each other. (People who are color-blind may not be able to distinguish between them.)

- Use color to highlight data. For example, format positive numbers in blue and format negative numbers in red.

- Resist the temptation to overload your publications with color. Instead, select color to focus attention on a few key areas.

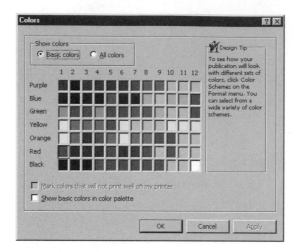

The pure color options ────────►
Because the selected color is pure red, Publisher displays an expanded palette of basic colors with the selected color surrounded by a black box.

7. Select the red in column 8 and click OK.

8. Click the arrow to the right of the New box in the Accent 2 row, click More Colors, click the orange in column 6 of the orange row, and click OK.

9. Click the arrow to the right of the New box in the Accent 3 row and click More Colors. You see these options:

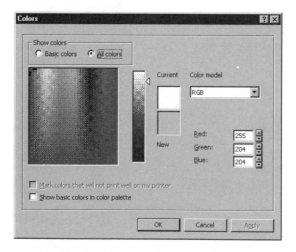

The color scale ────────►
Because Accent 3 is not a pure color, Publisher displays a color scale so that you can select precisely the color you want.

10. Half-hidden at the top of the color scale is a cross hair. Point to it and drag it anywhere in the box. When you release the mouse button, Publisher displays the color you've selected in the New box, analyzes its red, green, and blue content, and identifies the luminance (intensity) on the vertical scale to the right of the color scale.

Changing the color

11. Now point to the arrow next to the vertical luminance scale and drag it up and down, noting the changes in the New box.

Changing the intensity

12. Take a little time to explore this version of the Colors dialog box further. Then, when you're ready, use the arrows at the end of the Red, Green, and Blue boxes (or type the numbers directly) to specify the settings shown here:

Red   *106*
Green   *161*
Blue   *104*

As you enter each setting, the positions of the cross hair and the vertical luminance scale arrow change, as does the color in the New box.

13. Click OK to return to the Color Scheme dialog box.

14. Click the arrow to the right of the New box in the Accent 4 row, and click More Colors. Then click the Basic Colors option, click the brown in column 3 of the orange row, and click OK twice to return to the press release template.

Elements in the publication that were already formatted with one of the scheme colors are updated with the corresponding new colors. Let's apply the new color scheme to a few other elements in the template before you use it:

1. Select the *PRESS RELEASE* banner text, click the Font Color button, and change the color to green.

2. Select the row of dots in the first column, click the Fill Color button on the Formatting toolbar, and change the color to red. (Initially, only one of the dots changes to the new color, but when you click outside the selection, the color of all the dots is updated.)

Changing hue and saturation

In some programs, you create a color by changing the settings for hue, saturation, and luminance. When you create a custom color in Publisher, you can change the hue and saturation of the color by simply dragging the cross hair in the color scale. To change the hue, simply drag the cross hair horizontally across the scale. To change the saturation, drag the cross hair vertically.

3. Press Ctrl+M to move to the background, select the sun graphic, and right-click it. Choose Change Picture and then Recolor Picture from the shortcut menu to display the dialog box shown earlier on page 87.

4. Select orange from the Color drop-down list and click OK.

5. Return to the foreground and change the zoom setting to Whole Page to get a bird's-eye view of the new color scheme in place, as shown here:

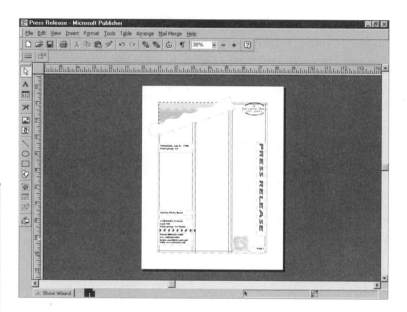

Although you have made only a couple of changes to the color scheme for the press release template, you have selected colors that complement one another. Before you start creating color schemes on your own, be sure to read the tip about the effect of color on page 139.

Creating a Publication Based on a Custom Template

After all that work, you're probably anxious to use your custom template to create an actual publication. Let's put the template to the test:

1. With the Press Release template open, click the Save button and then choose Close from the File menu.

2. Choose New from the File menu and then click the Templates button at the bottom of the Catalog dialog box to display this dialog box:

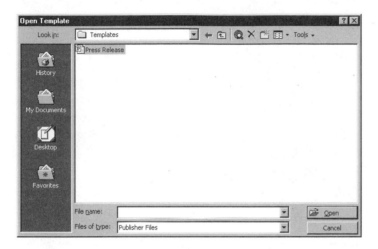

3. Double-click Press Release to open a new publication that uses the Press Release template.

4. Choose Save As from the File menu and then save the file in the My Documents folder with the name *Fossil Tour Press Release*.

Saving a template-based publication

Now you're ready to add some text to the press release. For this example, you'll insert enough placeholder text to necessitate adding a second page, which will enable you to see the background elements in action. For the text, let's use the paragraph from the newsletter. Follow these steps:

1. Open Newsletter, select the first paragraph of the fossil dig tour story, and click the Copy button.

2. Open Fossil Tour Press Release, clicking No if Publisher asks if you want to save changes to the Newsletter file.

3. Draw a text frame between the date and contact frames that stretches across the page to the left edge of the *PRESS RE-LEASE* banner.

4. With the insertion point in the new frame, click the Paste button and press Enter.

5. Repeat step 4 four more times. The press release looks something like this:

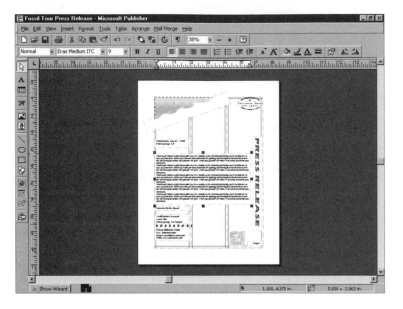

Now let's add the second page and insert a page of text:

Inserting a page

1. Choose Page from the Insert menu to display this dialog box:

2. Check that After Current Page is selected and then click OK to display a new page.

3. Draw another text frame that takes up most of the page and obscures a significant portion of the graphic at the bottom of the page.

4. Press F9 to zoom to 100%, copy the placeholder paragraph from page 1, and paste it into the new text frame on page 2 enough times to fill the frame.

5. With the text frame still selected, press Ctrl+T to make the frame transparent. As you can see here, the graphic now shows through the frame:

Making text frames transparent

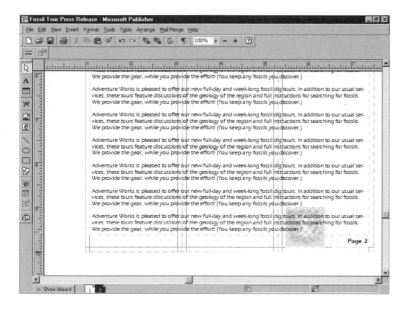

6. To see the new press release on paper, click the Print button. Then save and close the publication.

Now you can put your skills and creative energy to work designing your own templates.

More About Printing and Publishing

In this chapter, you look at more ways to fine-tune and proof your files, as well as how to handle final page adjustments. Then you create materials for bulk mailings and prepare a publication for commercial printing. Finally, you use a wizard to create a Web page.

The techniques you learn in this chapter help you make your publications available to a much wider audience, whether you are creating a flyer, brochure, or postcard.

Publications created and concepts covered:

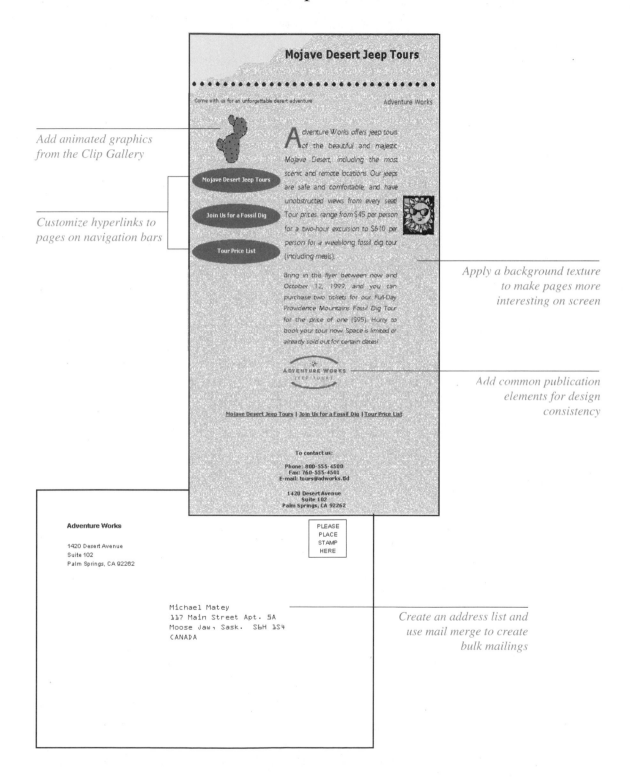

Add animated graphics from the Clip Gallery

Customize hyperlinks to pages on navigation bars

Apply a background texture to make pages more interesting on screen

Add common publication elements for design consistency

Create an address list and use mail merge to create bulk mailings

Up to this point, you have created several types of publications. Along the way, we have shown you how to fine-tune their contents, design, and color schemes. After all that hard work, you want things to run smoothly when you are ready to print.

In earlier chapters, you simply clicked the Print button to print one copy of a publication. But usually your printing needs will be much more complex. In this chapter, we show you how to prepare a publication for printing on your own printer or by a printing service. We also show you how to prepare bulk mailings. Finally, you use the Web Site Wizard to create a publication that can be published on a Web server and viewed with a Web browser.

Making Final Adjustments

It is very difficult to produce a completely error-free publication. Whether you are printing 1000, 100, or even 10 copies of a publication, and whether you are printing with your own printer or with a commercial printing service, you can wind up wasting a lot of time, money, and resources if you don't carefully look over the pages of a publication before committing it to paper. Follow these guidelines to catch most errors:

- **On-screen proof.** Look over the publication on the screen at 100% to verify that it includes all the necessary information and that each component is correctly placed.

- **Paper proof.** Print a proof copy of the publication and read everything carefully, checking for spelling and grammatical errors as well as incorrect information. In spite of all the advantages of online proofing, errors are often missed on the screen but caught on paper. When we showed you how to spell-check a publication on page 27, we cautioned that you cannot depend on spell-checking and grammar-checking to catch all your mistakes. Always read the publication word-for-word before distributing it, and if you don't trust your skills in this area, ask someone else to read it, too.

- **Proofing checklist.** For a complex publication, make a checklist of things to look for. (See the adjacent tip for suggested checklist items.) Then check each item on the list separately.

Making a checklist

When proofing a publication before the final printing, you should maintain a checklist of items to look for and then check each item on the list separately. Although your particular needs may vary depending on the type of publication, certain things should always be checked. First scrutinize all the different elements in your publication for consistency of style, formatting, capitalization, etc. Next double-check the accuracy of certain key elements like names, phone numbers, addresses, and page references. Finally, check the placement and alignment of items on each page. (As you check placement, you should also make sure that nothing is missing from the page.)

If you try to look for too many items at once, you are bound to miss something.

For practice, you'll scrutinize the postcard you created in Chapter 1 as you prepare it for printing. You'll also make any necessary page-setup adjustments. Follow these steps:

1. If necessary, start Publisher. Then either click the Existing Files button in the Catalog dialog box or click the Open button on the Standard toolbar. Either way, the Open Publication dialog box appears. Double-click Postcard to display it in the work area.

2. Take a look at each element on the postcard, check its placement on the page, and read through the text to check for errors. ← Proofreading

Everything seems OK, except that the bottom right corner of the postcard looks empty. Since you first created this publication, you have developed a logo for Adventure Works. Let's add the logo to the empty corner:

1. Copy and paste the logo from Brochure into Postcard. Then move the logo to the bottom right corner of the postcard.

2. Select *Adventure Works* and change the text size to 9. Then resize the frame until it is about 1 inch high and the same width as the phone/fax/e-mail frame above it.

3. Next select *Adventure Works* in the oval frame and change the text size to 10 so that it shows up better. The postcard now looks like the one shown at the top of the next page.

Design Checker

Publisher includes the Design Checker, which you can use to look over your publications for any potential design problems. To activate this feature, choose Design Checker from the Tools menu. In the Design Checker dialog box, designate whether you want all or a range of pages checked and whether or not you want to check the background pages. To see the Design Checker's checklist, click the Options button. Here, you can select or deselect options such as checking for empty frames, text in the overflow area, covered objects, and distorted graphics. When you have made your selections, click OK twice to begin the check. If Design Checker finds any problems, it selects the object and displays a message box describing the problem. If you click Explain, Publisher displays a help topic with more information about the problem. Otherwise, you can click Ignore or Ignore All to leave the object as is or you can fix the problem and then click Continue. When the design check is complete, click OK. You can't rely on Design Checker to locate all design-related errors in your publications, so be sure to scrutinize them carefully yourself before printing them.

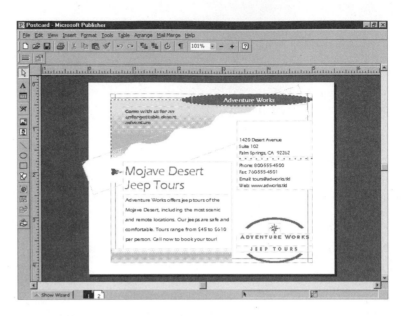

Adjusting the Page Setup

Ideally, you want to have the page setup of a publication settled before you begin to work on it. However, sometimes you make adjustments later, and you then need to make sure the adjustments haven't created any problems. Suppose you are sending the postcard to a printing service, and you learn that you can save money if you change the size of the publication from 5.5 by 4.25 inches to 5.85 by 4.13 inches. Let's make the change and fix any problems it might cause:

Changing the size of a publication

1. Choose Page Setup from the File menu to show this dialog box:

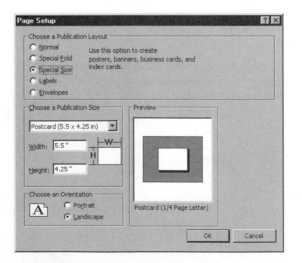

This dialog box shows that Postcard has been set up in a special size format. In the Choose A Publication Layout section, you can select another layout type if necessary. You can change the orientation from landscape to portrait in the Choose An Orientation section.

2. Click the arrow to the right of the Choose A Publication Size box and select Postcard (5.85 by 4.13 in). Publisher updates the Preview box and changes the measurements displayed in the Width and Height boxes. (If you need to enter a custom size specification, you can enter numbers in these boxes.)

3. Click OK to update the page setup of the postcard, like this:

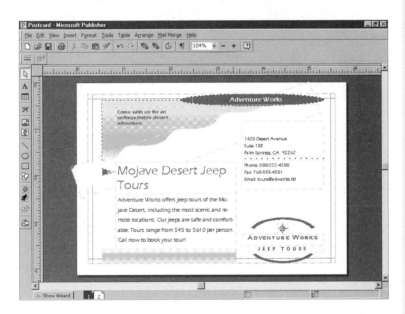

Looking over the elements of the postcard, you should notice that the title and main text paragraph now wrap differently, and the Web address no longer fits in its frame. Also, the gold blocks, the blue oval, and the logo no longer reach the edges of the postcard. Follow these steps to fix these problems:

1. In the title, click an insertion point to the left of the *J* in *Jeep* and press Shift+Enter to rebreak the first line.

2. Select the frame of the main text paragraph and drag the right middle handle to the right until the lines rewrap to eliminate the hyphens. Resize the title frame to match the main text frame.

Printing odd-sized publications

If you print publications that are smaller or larger than a standard piece of paper, such as business cards or banners, you can adjust the printing options. For a smaller publication, choose Print from the File menu and click the Page Options button. To print one copy of the publication per page, select the Print One Copy Per Sheet option. To print multiple copies, click the Print Multiple Copies option. To customize this setting further, click the Custom Options button. To restore the default settings in this dialog box, click the Automatically Calculate Spacing check box. To print a large publication, choose Print from the File menu and click the Tile Printing Options button to display the Poster And Banner Printing Options dialog box. With the Print Entire Page option selected, Publisher shows how many pages it will take to print an entire publication. To change how much each tile (or page) will overlap another, enter a number in the Overlap Tiles By edit box. To print only part of the publication, click the Print One Tile From Ruler Origin option. By default, Publisher prints from the zero on the ruler, so it will print the first part of the publication. To print a different part, change the zero origin on the ruler first. (See the tip on page 47.)

3. Resize the phone/fax/e-mail frame to display the Web address.

4. Reposition the two gold blocks so that they align with the pink guide on the left. Then reposition the blue oval and the logo so that they align with the pink guide on the right.

5. To maintain the balance of the design, also realign the address, dots, and phone/fax/e-mail frames with the right guide.

6. Save the file. Here are the results:

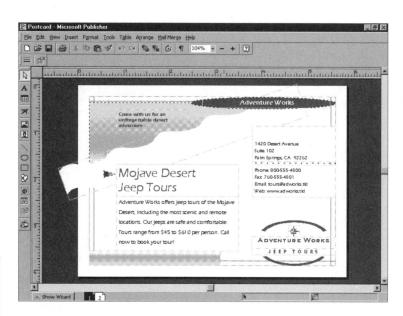

The Print Troubleshooter

To help you identify potential printing problems, Publisher provides the Print Troubleshooter. You can tell Publisher to activate Print Troubleshooter every time you print by choosing Options from the Tools menu, clicking the Print tab, selecting the Automatically Display Print Troubleshooter check box, and clicking OK. If you prefer to activate the feature only when you need it, choose Print Troubleshooter from the Help menu. You can then select from the list of potential problems and read through the help topics to try to locate a solution.

Printing Mass Mailings

If you keep a mailing list of customers, club members, or other contacts and you want to send the same postcard or brochure to all of them, you don't have to address and print each one in turn. You can use Publisher's *mail merge* feature to print a set of similar documents ready for bulk mailing.

The mail merge process involves two documents. You create one document called the *main publication* that contains the information that does not change from printout to printout—for example, the text and graphics of the postcard. In the main publication, you insert placeholders called *merge fields* for the information that does change—for example, the name and address of each person you want to receive the postcard. (You can also insert codes that control the merging process.) You create another document called the *data source* that is essentially a database of the variable information. For this example, you'll use the postcard you have already created as your main publication, but you need to create a data source. Then you can merge the two files together to print a set of publications ready for bulk mailing.

Creating the Data Source

If you already have a list that you want to use for bulk mailings, you don't have to recreate it. You can use it with Publisher's mail merge process (see the tip on the next page). If you don't already have a list, Publisher can guide you through the steps for creating one, like this:

1. With Postcard open, choose Create Publisher Address List from the Mail Merge menu to display the dialog box shown below. (You may need to install the Mail Merge feature first.)

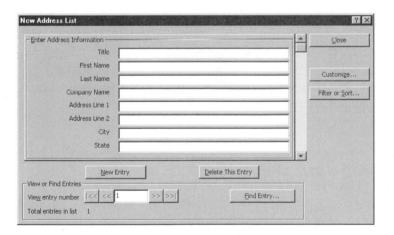

Publisher lists all the commonly used merge field names in the Enter Address Information section. To add an entry, simply type in the appropriate boxes. Or, you can customize the field names for your particular needs.

2. Click the Customize button to display the dialog box shown on the next page.

Data source decisions

Before creating the data source for a mail merge publication, you should think through how the data source will be used. If you plan on sorting any of your data (see the tip on page 156), you need to put the information you want to sort in separate fields. If you think you may use the data source for different kinds of mail merge publications, then you may want to add extra fields that won't be used in one type of publication but will in another. For example, in an address label publication, you may want to include a job title, such as *Sandy Rhodes, President*, but in the salutation of a letter, you may only want to include the first and/or last name (*Dear Sandy Rhodes:* or *Dear Sandy:*). You'll have more flexibility if you include all the information but organize it in separate fields.

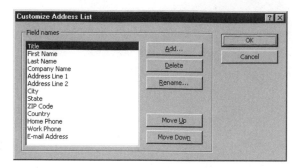

Removing fields

3. With Title selected in the list, click the Delete button and then click Yes to confirm the deletion. Publisher removes this field from the list.

4. Next repeat the previous step to remove the Company Name, Home Phone, Work Phone, and E-mail Address fields from the list.

5. Click OK to return to the New Address List dialog box with the updated list of field names.

6. Enter the information shown in the table on the facing page, pressing either Tab or Enter to move from field to field. After you fill in the last field in one entry, click the New Entry button or press Enter to move to a new entry. You can use the arrows on either side of the View Entry Number box to move back and forth through the entries.

More ways to customize field names

To adjust the field name list, use the Customize Address List dialog box. To add a new field, click the Add button, type a name for the new field, decide if you want it to appear before or after the selected field, and then click OK. To rename a field, select it, type a new name, and click OK. To change the field order to match the order in which you enter data, use the Move Up and Move Down buttons.

Using a data source created in another program

If you already have a suitable table of information set up in another program, you may be able to use that existing file as the data source for your merged publications. First click an insertion point in the text frame where you want your merge fields to appear. Next choose Open Data Source from the Mail Merge menu, select the Merge Information From Another Type Of File option to display the Open Data Source dialog box, and then select the file you want to use. (The information in the file must be set up in a table or be separated by tabs or commas for Publisher to be able to use it as mail merge data source.) Publisher can use existing database information created in certain versions of Microsoft Access, Microsoft Word, Microsoft Works, Microsoft Excel, Paradox, and dBASE.

Field	Entry 1	Entry 2	Entry 3
First Name	*Erik*	*Michael*	*Dale*
Last Name	*Gavriluk*	*Matey*	*Washburn*
Address Line 1	*1504 14th Avenue SW*	*117 Main Street*	*1301 Brookline Road*
Address Line 2		*Apt. 5A*	
City	*Great Falls*	*Moose Jaw*	*San Luis Obispo*
State	*MT*	*Sask.*	*CA*
ZIP Code	*59404*	*S6H 1S4*	*93401*
Country		*CANADA*	

7. After adding the three entries, click Close. When Publisher displays the Save As dialog box, save the file as *Data Source* in the My Documents folder.

Completing the Main Publication

The back of the postcard includes an address frame but does not include the merge fields you need to complete the mail merge process. Let's add them now:

1. First move to page 2 of Postcard and select the text in the address frame. ◄   *Entering merge fields*

2. Choose Open Data Source from the Mail Merge menu to display this dialog box:

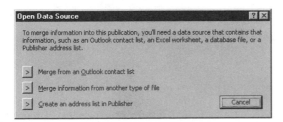

3. Since you have already created the data source, click the arrow to the left of the second option. When Publisher displays the Open Data Source dialog box, simply double-click Data Source. You then see the dialog box shown at the top of the following page.

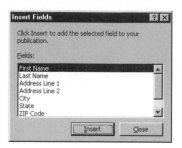

4. With First Name selected, click the Insert button to insert the merge field into the address frame. (If necessary, drag the dialog box out of the way so that you can see the results.)

5. With the insertion point to the right of the merge field, press the Spacebar once, and double-click Last Name in the Insert dialog box to add that merge field to the address frame.

6. Next press Enter, add the Address Line 1 merge field, press the Spacebar, and then add the Address Line 2 merge field.

7. Press Enter, add the City merge field, type a comma and a space, add the State merge field, type two spaces, and add the ZIP Code merge field.

8. Finally, press Enter, add the Country merge field, and then click Close. Here are the results:

Filtering and sorting data

If your data source contains many entries and you want to merge only those entries that meet certain criteria (for example, only those with specific zip codes), you can "filter" the entries to extract the ones you want. Choose Filter And Sort from the Mail Merge menu. On the Filter tab, select a field and a comparison setting, and then type the value to compare the field to. (You can enter up to three different filter settings.) To sort the information contained in your data source in a particular order, click the Sort tab of the Filtering And Sorting dialog box. Select the field you want to sort by and then click the Ascending option to sort from lowest to highest or the Descending option to sort from highest to lowest. (You can enter up to three different sort settings.) To redisplay the entire data source, click the Remove Filter or Remove Sort button on the appropriate tab of the Filtering And Sorting dialog box and then click OK.

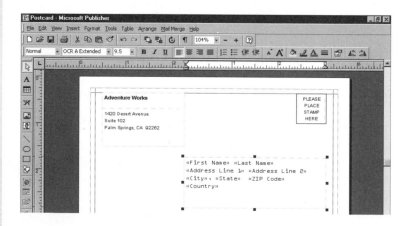

For this example, you inserted the merge fields in the order in which they appear in the list. However, you can insert them in any order or any combination. You can also manually rearrange merge fields after you have added them to a publication.

Merging the Publications

Now you are ready to merge the main publication with the data source so that you can print the postcards. Try this:

1. Choose Merge from the Mail Merge menu. Publisher merges the files and displays the name and address information for the first entry, along with the Preview Data dialog box.

2. Drag the dialog box out of the way and click the Next Entry button (>>) to see the information for the second entry, like this:

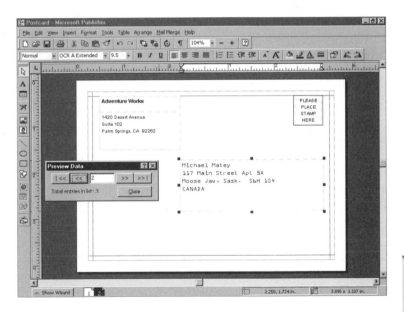

3. Click the Next Entry button once more to view the third entry.

4. When you are finished previewing the data, click the Close button. The postcard now displays only the merge field placeholders. (You can preview the merge results at any time by choosing Show Merge Results from the Mail Merge menu.)

   If you need to make adjustments to the placement of the merge fields, you can do so directly on the page. If you need to edit the data-source entries or add more entries, choose Edit Publisher Address List from the Mail Merge menu, open the data source, and make the changes. When you are confident that the merge process produces a flawless set of publications, you can print them. Follow the steps on the next page.

Printing labels and envelopes

Publisher can create several types of labels and envelopes with the mail merge feature. To create a label or envelope publication, choose the style you want in the Labels or Envelopes category of the Catalog dialog box. If the category does not list the label or envelope size you need, you can select a different one from the Page Setup dialog box. You can then enter merge fields in the publication and format them as usual. For specific information on how to print envelopes or labels, see Publisher's Help feature.

Printing the merged
publications

1. Choose Print Merge from the File menu to display a modified version of the Print dialog box.

2. Next click OK to print all three merged postcards. (You can also click the Test button to print just the first entry of a merged publication to check that everything looks fine.)

Sending a Publication to a Printing Service

For a few business forms, flyers, or labels, your own printer may have enough features to get the job done. But under the following circumstances, you will need to enlist the help of a printing service, such as a copy shop or commercial printer:

- **Quality.** You need a more polished, professional look than your printer can produce. Printing services have the capacity to print in full color at a much higher quality than standard office or home printers.

- **Print run.** The data source contains enough entries that using a printing service is more economical, especially when you factor in such considerations as the wear and tear on your own printer and the time it will take you to supervise the printing.

- **Special paper or size.** The publication you want to print requires special paper, such as card stock for a postcard, that your printer can't handle. Or economies of scale can be achieved if several copies are printed at a time on large sheets of paper that won't fit in your printer's paper tray.

The decisions involved in preparing a publication for outside printing are often far more complex than those for printing on your own printer. However, Publisher can help you with the task of preparing your publications for a printing service. We can't cover all the details in this section, but we do want to quickly outline the tasks that Publisher recommends you complete to maximize your chances of success. As you read through the tasks, bear in mind that you should complete them in order. Because the first four tasks affect the look of a publication, ideally you should tackle them before you even begin to work on the publication itself. For more detailed information about these tasks, we strongly urge you to search the Help feature's index for the *service bureaus* topics and read the advice given in all the topics that relate to your situation. (See the tip below.)

- **Type of printing.** Find out which types are available and which type best suits the needs of your publication.

- **Printing service.** Shop around and choose which one you will use based not only on price but on your feelings about the level of service (help) you will receive.

- **Publication details.** Visit the printing service you select and discuss the details of your publication.

- **Set up.** Set up your computer and your publication according to the printing service's instructions for the type of printing you have selected. For example, you may need to install the driver (control program) for a different printer and finalize your publication with that printer selected in the Print Setup dialog box (even though that printer is not physically connected to your computer).

- **Proofreading.** Check the publication the same way you would before printing it on your own printer (see page 148).

- **File preparation.** Prepare the publication file for delivery to the printing service.

- **File delivery.** Finally, deliver your publication.

As an example, suppose you want to send the flyer you created in Chapter 2 to an outside printing service. Assuming that you have already taken care of the first five tasks and that you are now ready to have Publisher prepare the flyer file on a floppy disk for delivery to the printing service, follow these steps:

1. Open Flyer and insert a blank disk in your floppy drive.

2. Choose Pack And Go and then Take To A Commercial Printing Service from the File menu to display the Pack And Go Wizard's first dialog box, as shown on the next page.

A quick overview

To get a quick overview of what it takes to prepare a Publisher document for a commercial printing service, click the Contents tab of the Help Window and click the *Print Publications* category. Then click the *Print your publication at a commercial printing service* subcategory and read each of the four available topics. You should also read about how Publisher handles color; check out the topic entitled *About process-color and spot-color printing*.

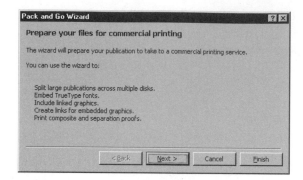

3. Click Next to display this dialog box:

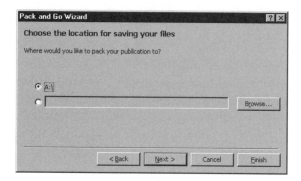

4. Click Next again to display this dialog box:

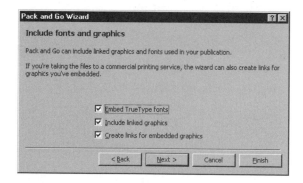

No missing pieces

5. The flyer is very simple, but to ensure that the file doesn't arrive at the printing service with missing pieces, leave all the options selected so that Publisher will include everything that's needed. Then click Next to display the dialog box shown at the top of the facing page.

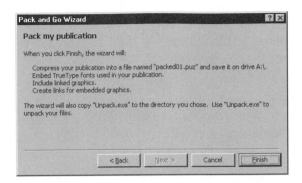

6. Click Finish. The wizard goes to work, storing everything the printing service will need on the floppy disk, including the Unpack.exe file, which the service will use to unpack the file on its computer. When the wizard is finished, you see this message:

Copying to a floppy disk

7. Click OK to close the wizard and print a copy of the flyer on your own printer. Then save and close the file.

Publishing on the Web

If you need to create Web pages for your organization's Web site or intranet, or if you want to create pages for your own Web site, you can design the pages as publications and then have Publisher convert them to the necessary HTML (Hyper-Text Markup Language) format. You don't need to know anything about HTML, because Publisher takes care of the coding for you behind the scenes. If you don't have access to the Internet or don't have any need to create a Web page, you can just skim through this section to get an idea of Publisher's capabilities.

HyperText Markup Language (HTML)

Creating a Web Site

As with other types of publications, you can use a wizard to guide you through the process of creating Web pages or you can create them from scratch. In this section, you will create a page for Adventure Works using the Web Site Wizard, which helps you generate a professional-looking Web page with very little effort. Let's fire up the wizard now:

The Web Site Wizard

1. With Publisher started, choose New from the File menu to display the Catalog dialog box.

2. Click the Web Sites category, scroll through the list in the right pane, and double-click Waves Web Site to start the wizard.

3. Click Next to move to the color scheme dialog box and with Tropics selected, click Next again to display this dialog box:

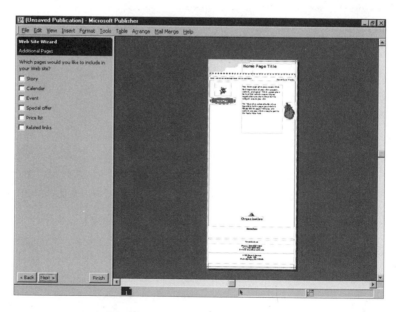

Adding pages

4. From the various additional pages you can add to your Web site, such as calendars, special offers, and order forms, select Story and Price List and then click Next.

5. With None selected as the form option, click Next.

6. Check that Both A Vertical And Horizontal Bar is selected and click Next.

7. Check that No is selected as the sound option and click Next. (See the tip on page 166 for information about adding sound.)

8. Click Yes as the texture option and click Next.

9. Check that Primary Business is selected as the personal information set and click Finish.

10. Click the Hide Wizard button and change the zoom setting to 100% to display these results:

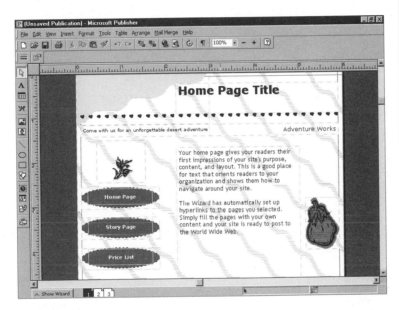

Publisher displays the first page of the Web site, called the *home page*, which includes text and graphic placeholders. To move to another page of the Web site, you can click the buttons in the page controls as usual.

11. Save the file as *Web Site* in the My Documents folder.

Now you can start filling in all the placeholder text. Luckily, you use the same techniques to work with text and objects in a Web page as you do when you are working with them in other publications. Follow these steps:

1. Select the Home Page Title placeholder and type *Mojave Desert Jeep Tours*. Then select the text and change the font size to 16 so that it sits on one line.

Converting publications into Web pages and vice versa

With Publisher, you can convert a publication into a Web site or convert a Publisher-designed Web site into certain publication types. To turn a publication into a Web site, first open the publication and then choose Create Web Site From Current Publication from the File menu. Next decide if you want the wizard to create the design and then click OK. If you select the second option, Publisher prompts you to run Design Checker (see the tip on page 149). To turn a Publisher-designed Web site into a regular publication, first open the Web site file in Publisher. Then click the Show Wizard button and select the Convert To Print option from the top pane. In the bottom pane, select the type of publication you want to create. (You can select either a newsletter or a brochure.) Publisher asks if you want to save changes to the Web site, closes it, and then opens a new publication of the specified type. If certain elements do not fit the new type, Publisher moves them to the Extra Content tab of the Design Gallery. (Click the Extra Content button in the wizard's pane to view them.)

Inserting animated graphics

2. Double-click the first graphic (the flower) on the home page to display the Clip Gallery window and then click the Motion Clips tab. (The graphics stored on this tab are animated so that when you view them in a Web browser, they move or change in some other way.)

The Play Clip button

3. Click the cactus graphic, and then click the Play Clip button.

4. When Publisher opens a small preview window, watch as the cactus sprouts flowers, and then click the window's Close button.

5. Click the graphic again, click Insert Clip, and then close the Clip Gallery window.

6. Now double-click the second placeholder graphic and replace it with something more appropriate. (We inserted the sun graphic used in other Adventure Works publications.)

7. Save Web Site, open the Flyer publication, and copy both paragraphs of the main text. Then reopen Web Site and paste the paragraphs into the text frame on the home page.

8. Click No when Publisher asks if you want to use autoflow and then resize the frame until it is long enough to fit all of the text. Here are the results at 66%:

Overlapping objects

Whenever possible, you should avoid overlapping frames on Web pages. Publisher treats the overlapping objects as one item by creating a rectangular area, called a *graphic region*, that contains them. Graphic regions are downloaded as one graphic and take more time to appear than separate objects. Publisher alerts you if objects are overlapping by displaying a thick red border around the graphic region. If you feel the effect is worth the longer download time, you can leave it as it is. However, don't overlap form controls, because they will not function properly. (See the tip on page 169 for more information on forms in Web pages.)

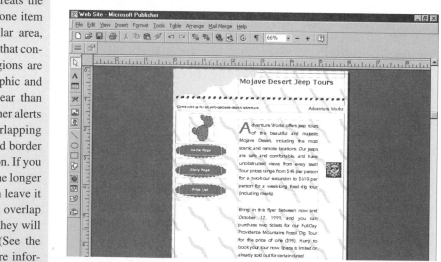

9. Before you move on, scroll to the bottom of the home page and replace the logo placeholder with the logo from Brochure.

Now let's fill in the second page of the Web site:

1. Move to page 2, replace the title with *Join Us for a Fossil Dig*, and replace the placeholder story text with the paragraphs you copied from the flyer.

2. Select the quote placeholder text in the box on the left and type *"Our fossil dig tours are one-of-a-kind in the Mojave Desert area." Sandy Rhodes, Owner of Adventure Works.*

3. As a final touch for this page, add an appropriate graphic and caption. Here are the results:

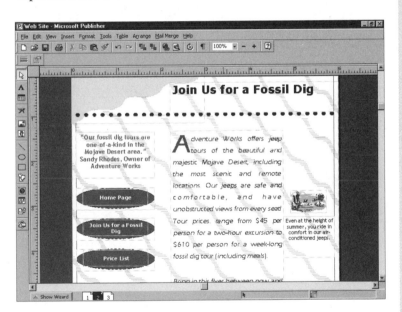

Now you are ready to fill in the final page of the Web site. To speed up the process, you can reuse the information you entered in the table of the price list brochure. Follow these steps:

1. Save the Web site and then open the Brochure publication.

2. Move to the page with the price list table and click it once to select it.

3. Choose Select and then Table from the Table menu. Then click the Copy button.

Adding sound or video

You may want to add sound or video files to a publication that will be viewed on the Internet or on an intranet. To add a background sound to a Web page, choose Web Properties from the File menu and then click the Page tab. In the Background Sound section, enter the path of the sound you want to use in the File Name edit box, or click the Browse button and navigate to the file you want to use. Next click the Loop Forever option to have the background sound play continuously or click the Loop option and enter the number of times you want the sound to play. Then click OK. To hear the sound, preview the Web site in your browser. To insert a video file, you can use an animated Clip Gallery file as you did on page 164 or insert another file by choosing Picture and then From File from the Insert menu. Navigate to the file you want and then double-click it to add it to the Web page. You can then move and resize it as usual. As with sound, you will have to preview the Web site in your browser to see the video file.

4. Open Web Site, move to page 3, and scroll the top of the table into view.

5. Click the first cell of the table, click the Paste button, and then click Yes when Publisher asks if you want to extend the table.

6. Scroll to the bottom of the table, which has been extended so that it overlaps the second table on the page. Delete the unused rows of the first table, and then delete the second table.

7. Delete the line breaks from rows two through five so that the tour descriptions are just one line long.

8. Resize the first and second columns as necessary so that all of the tour descriptions appear on one line. (See page 113 if you need help resizing columns.) The table now looks this:

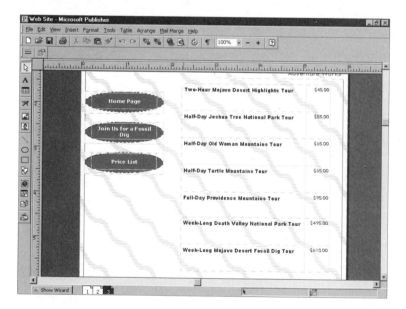

9. Scroll to the top of the page and replace the title with *Tour Price List*.

10. Next scroll to the bottom of the page and copy and paste the logo from page 1.

11. Save the Web site.

When the Web Site Wizard set up this publication, it included three *hyperlinks* on *navigation bars* that you can click to move

Hyperlinks and
navigation bars

from one page to another within the Web site. Follow these steps to take a closer look at these hyperlinks:

1. Move to page 1 and notice that the second and third hyperlinks have been updated to reflect the new titles of their pages, but the first hyperlink still reads *Home Page*. (The same pattern is followed on all three pages.) Select *Home Page* in the first blue oval and type *Mojave Desert Jeep Tours*.

2. Click any of the ovals to select the group and then resize the group's frame until the text in all three hyperlink buttons fits on one line. Here are the results at 100%:

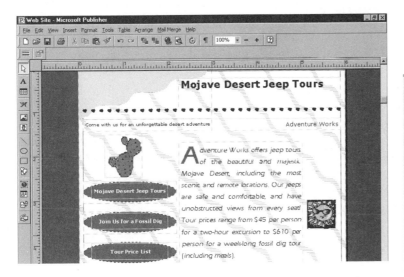

3. Move to page 2 and notice that although the hyperlink text has been updated, the oval sizes have not. Resize them now.

4. Repeat this step for page 3.

Adjusting Color and Background

As with other publications, you are not stuck with the design or color scheme you have chosen for the Web Site publication. Often you will want to customize the color scheme or change the background color or texture. Suppose you want to change the background texture to something more appropriate for Adventure Works. Follow the steps on the following page to adjust the background.

Adding hyperlinks

To add a text hyperlink, first select the text that you want to convert to a hyperlink. Next click the Insert Hyperlink button on the Standard toolbar. In the Create A Hyperlink To section of the Hyperlink dialog box, select the appropriate option. Then type the address of the hyperlink (or select the appropriate page option if your hyperlink moves you to another page within the same Web site) and click OK. Publisher underlines the text and changes it to the appropriate hyperlink color. To add an object hyperlink, select the object and then follow the same procedure. To add a hyperlink using part of an object, click the Hot Spot Tool button on the Objects toolbar and draw a frame over the part of the object that you want to activate. Publisher then displays the Hyperlink dialog box, where you specify the options you want as usual.

1. Move to page 1 of Web Site and choose Color And Background Scheme from the Format menu to display this dialog box:

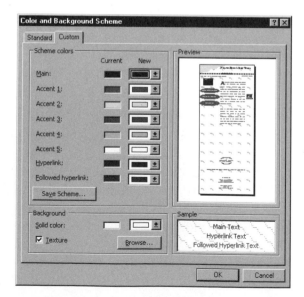

On the Standard tab, you can change to a different color scheme, change the background color, and apply a different texture. Publisher then displays the results in the adjacent Preview box so that you can get an idea of what the change will look like.

2. Click the Custom tab to display these options:

Slow Web pages

Think twice before you add too many graphic gizmos to a Web page. Though graphic effects like textured backgrounds can enliven a Web page, they can muddy your message, and they also take longer to download. If you think speed is going to be important to your viewers, you may want to stick to a solid color background.

Here, you can change any one of the scheme colors as well as the colors assigned to hyperlink text before and after the viewer has clicked the link.

3. To change the background texture, click the Browse button in the Background section to display this dialog box:

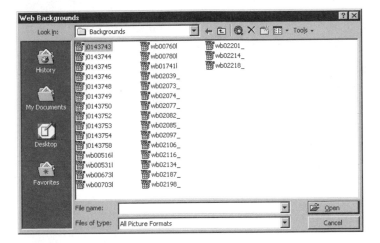

4. Not very informative! Click the arrow to the right of the Views button on the toolbar. Select Preview from the drop-down list to open a preview pane on the right side of the dialog box, where a sample of the selected background is displayed.

The Views button

5. Select a few backgrounds to see what's available. Finish by selecting Wb007601 (a pattern that resembles sand) and clicking Open to return to the Color And Background Scheme dialog box. Then click OK to see the results shown on the following page.

Web page forms

The process of setting up a Web form so that it retrieves information correctly can be tricky and time-consuming. Before you attempt to set up a Web form in Publisher, you might want to contact your Internet service provider (ISP) for more information about their requirements. If the form you need is somewhat complex, you may be better off creating the Web page in a more sophisticated Web-design program, such as Microsoft FrontPage. If you want to add a simple form to a Web page in Publisher, click the Form Control button on the Objects toolbar and choose one of the form control types from the drop-down menu. (For more information about the different types of form controls, see Publisher's Help feature.) You can then draw a frame for the control, enter your form's information, and move and format the control as usual. (To ensure that the form works properly, do not overlap any form control frames.)

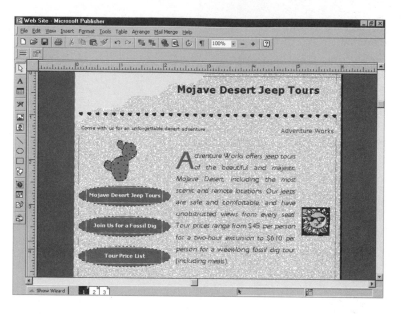

Previewing a Web Page

When you create a publication that you will print on paper, you can see all the elements on the screen pretty much the way they will look on paper. However, when you create a Web site, Publisher can't show you the dynamic elements, such as hyperlinks and moving graphics. It is important that you preview your Publisher-produced Web sites in a Web browser before publishing them for the world, or even others in your organization, to see. Let's look at the Adventure Works site:

Sending Web pages to a Web server

When you are ready to publish your Web site, you can use Publisher to guide you. With the Web site file open, choose Web Properties from the File menu. On the Site tab, you can enter keywords, separated by commas, which Web search engines will use to categorize your Web site. (For example, Adventure Works might enter *jeep, tours, Mojave Desert, fossil digs*.) In the Description box, enter a short description of your Web site's content. In the Target Audience section, select the type of browser you want and the language. Next click the Page tab, where you enter a filename for the home page of your Web site (usually, *index*) and designate the filename extension (check with your Internet service provider). When you are finished, click OK. To begin transmitting your Web files to your Internet service provider (ISP), choose Programs, Internet Explorer, and then Web Publishing Wizard from the Windows Start menu. Read through the wizard's instructions and enter the required information in each dialog box. (You will need to get this information from your ISP.) The wizard will then transmit the files using FTP to your ISP. (FTP stands for *File Transfer Protocol*.) If you prefer to use a different FTP program, choose Save As Web Page from the File menu, designate a folder in which to save your Web site, and click OK. You can then access the file and send it at any time. For more information, consult Publisher's Help feature and your ISP.

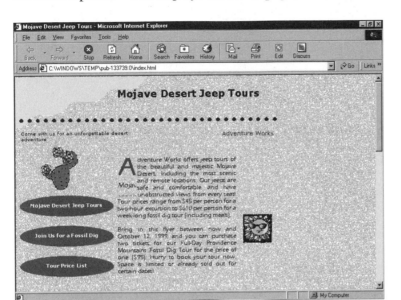

1. With Web Site open on your screen, click the Web Page Preview button on the Standard toolbar. After a few seconds, Publisher starts your Web browser—in our case, Microsoft Internet Explorer—and displays the home page, shown here:

2. Watch the animated graphic in action and then scroll through the page, checking all the elements carefully.

3. Next click the Join Us hyperlink button to check that it is linked to the correct page, and then click the Tour Price List button to move to that page.

4. When you finish looking over the Web site, simply click your browser's Close button to return to Publisher.

Depending on the Web browser you are using, various elements may appear differently than they do in Publisher. For example, text might be formatted differently or might wrap differently. If possible, view your Web site in more than one browser to be sure that it works for all your potential viewers; then make any necessary adjustments to the Publisher file. When you are ready to publish your Web site, read the facing tip.

That's the end of this chapter and of this Quick Course book. With the skills you've learned, you should be well on your way to producing exciting, professional-looking publications!

The Preview Troubleshooter

The Preview Troubleshooter helps you zero in on any potential problems with your Web site. To activate this feature, choose Options from the Tools menu and click the Preview Web Site With Preview Troubleshooter check box on the User Assistance tab and then click OK. When you click the Web Page Preview button, Publisher opens the Help window with the Preview Troubleshooter topic displayed. You can then use the Troubleshooter to identify and correct problems.

Index

Optimize
Microsoft® Office 2000
with multimedia training!

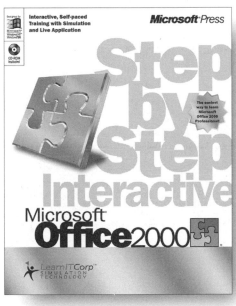

U.S.A.   **$29.99**
Canada $44.99
ISBN 0-7356-0506-8

MICROSOFT OFFICE 2000 STEP BY STEP INTERAC-TIVE is a multimedia learning system (in both audio and text versions) that shows you, through 20 to 30 hours of training, how to maximize the productivity potential of the Office 2000 programs: Microsoft Excel 2000, Word 2000, Access 2000, PowerPoint® 2000, Outlook® 2000, Publisher 2000, and Small Business Tools. If you already use Microsoft Office 97, this learning solution will help you make the transition to Office 2000 quickly and easily, and reach an even greater level of productivity.

Microsoft®

mspress.microsoft.com

See clearly—
now!

Here's the remarkable, *visual* way to quickly find answers about the powerfully integrated features of the Microsoft® Office 2000 applications. Microsoft Press AT A GLANCE books let you focus on particular tasks and show you, with clear, numbered steps, the easiest way to get them done right now. Put Office 2000 to work today, with AT A GLANCE learning solutions, made by Microsoft.

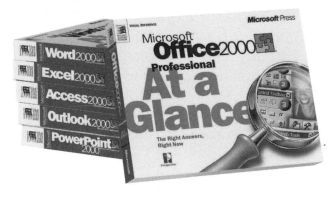

- MICROSOFT OFFICE 2000 PROFESSIONAL AT A GLANCE
- MICROSOFT WORD 2000 AT A GLANCE
- MICROSOFT EXCEL 2000 AT A GLANCE
- MICROSOFT POWERPOINT® 2000 AT A GLANCE
- MICROSOFT ACCESS 2000 AT A GLANCE
- MICROSOFT FRONTPAGE® 2000 AT A GLANCE
- MICROSOFT PUBLISHER 2000 AT A GLANCE
- MICROSOFT OFFICE 2000 SMALL BUSINESS AT A GLANCE
- MICROSOFT PHOTODRAW® 2000 AT A GLANCE
- MICROSOFT INTERNET EXPLORER 5 AT A GLANCE
- MICROSOFT OUTLOOK® 2000 AT A GLANCE

Microsoft®

mspress.microsoft.com

Register Today!

Return this
Quick Course® in Microsoft® Publisher 2000
registration card today

Microsoft Press
mspress.microsoft.com

OWNER REGISTRATION CARD   1-57231-990-9

Quick Course® in Microsoft® Publisher 2000

FIRST NAME   MIDDLE INITIAL   LAST NAME

INSTITUTION OR COMPANY NAME

ADDRESS

CITY   STATE   ZIP

E-MAIL ADDRESS   (   ) PHONE NUMBER

U.S. and Canada addresses only. Fill in information above and mail postage-free.
Please mail only the bottom half of this page.

For information about Microsoft Press®
products, visit our Web site at
mspress.microsoft.com

Microsoft·Press